800 Plus
Tiny Thoughts
For A
Bountiful Business

By

Rajendra K. Aneja

Winning Global Consumers
Leadership
Selling to Billions of Customers
Customer-Service
Power of Grocers
Managing Modern Retail
Harvesting Rural Markets
Planning and Controls
Business in Conflict-areas
Social Responsibility of Business

Dedicated To My Late Parents

Shri Hari Chand Aneja, and

Shrimati Prakash Kumari Aneja

and

My Brother

Narendra K. Aneja

THE INSPIRATION

"Seven social sins: politics without principles, wealth without work, pleasure without conscience, knowledge without character, commerce without morality, science without humanity, and worship without sacrifice."

- Mahatma Gandhi

BUSINESS, CONSCIENCE, BROTHERHOOD

"I believe that nothing can be greater than a business, however small it may be, that is governed by conscience; and that nothing can be meaner or more petty than a business, however large, governed without honesty and without brotherhood."

- Mr. William Lever, The First Viscount Leverhulme

FOLLOW YOUR HEART AND INTUITION

"Your time is limited, so don't waste it living someone else's life. Don't be trapped by dogma - which is living with the results of other people's thinking. Don't let the noise of others' opinions drown out your own inner voice. And most important, have the courage to follow your heart and intuition."

- Mr. Steve Jobs, Co-founder of Apple INC.

COURAGE AND CONFIDENCE

"Show, Courage and Confidence, Not Weakness."

- Hari Chand Aneja (Daddy)

ABOUT THIS BOOK

"Ghaghar mein Sagar", that is, "Insert the Ocean in a Pot", counselled my wise father many years ago, on my dilemma over the length of an article. My Dad's advice was also reinforced by two of the six rules of writing taught by the English novelist, Mr. George Orwell, "Never use a long word where a short one will do. If it is possible to cut a word out, always cut it out."

"Tiny Thoughts for a Bountiful Business", embraces 800 Plus pithy action ideas and guideposts, for Winning emerging global consumers, Selling to billions of customers, Leadership, Customer-Service, Power of grocers, Managing modern retail, Harvesting rural markets, Planning and controls, Business in conflict-areas, Social responsibility of business, etc., across nations.

Of the over 600,000 words, which I have published in my books, articles and Letters to the Editors, in the last 50 years and more, I have culled out these 800 Plus "Tiny Thoughts", which may lead to profits, prosperity and a munificent business.

I am grateful to my colleagues Amritaa Aneja, Gnanesh Mehta, Ashok Mishra and Payal Waghela for their contributions in suggesting ideas for the cover and for publishing this book. I am also grateful to Gnanesh Mehta for making a rich cover, showing a man enchanted with his bountiful business.

I hope that these 800 Plus "Tiny Thoughts" will help entrepreneurs, businessmen and managers to build strong businesses, and generate wealth for themselves, their employees and their countries.

ABOUT THE AUTHOR

Rajendra Aneja is the Managing Director of a Management Consulting Company providing services in Business Strategy, Retailing, Distribution Restructuring, Rural Marketing Feasibilities, Productivity, etc.

He worked with Unilever for 28 years in India, Latin America and Africa in a range of General Management, Marketing and Sales positions. He has worked on mass-markets in Brazil and later as Managing Director in Tanzania, Africa. He has dealt with a diverse range of products and assignments. He has been closely involved with Marketing and Sales strategy, Rural marketing, Customer-Service and Distribution restructuring projects in Brazil, Colombia, Venezuela, Peru, Ecuador, Sri Lanka and many other countries.

Rajendra Aneja has worked in the Middle East, as the CEO of a Retail group and of a Foods Company. He has worked on management assignments in India, Sri Lanka, Brazil, Colombia, Peru, Tanzania, Cote d'Ivoire, Senegal, Kenya, Egypt, Yemen, Kingdom of Saudi Arabia, Oman, etc., among other countries.

He was a Sir Dorabji Tata Scholar throughout his graduation from Sydenham College of Commerce and Economics and the Master's Degree in Management Studies from Jamnalal Bajaj Institute. He was also a Government of India Merit Scholar and received the Rotary Club Award for being the Best Student of the College. Subsequently he studied at the Harvard Business School and the Harvard Kennedy School of Government.

He has been frequently quoted by prestigious newspapers and magazines like the Financial Times (London), Fortune International (USA), Far Eastern Economic Review (Hong

Kong), Asia Inc. (Hong Kong), The McKinsey Quarterly (London), etc. The Economic Times wrote that he "is the brains behind the rural thrust of Hindustan Lever". The Asia Inc. (Hong Kong) commented that he "has achieved international recognition for his work in tapping Indian rural markets."

He has managed full semester courses on Marketing at the Jamnalal Bajaj Institute of Management Studies and the Sydenham College Management Institute, University of Mumbai.

He was also invited to speak by Kellogg School of Management, Chicago, USA, Tata Management Centre, the Glaxo Global CEOs' and Directors' Forum in London and Vietnam.

He has written eight other books, "Agenda for a New India", "Business Express: An Odyssey of Business Ideas, Sensitivities, Engagements & Emerging Global Consumers", "Conquer Rural Marketing Across Countries", "My Experiences in Modern Retail", "Little Thoughts for a Better World", "Slices & Spices of Life: From Rio to Manila via Mumbai, Dubai, etc.", "A Common Man Writes over One Thousand Letters to the Editor, Volume 1 & 2".

APPRECIATIONS

"You write very well. Aim to write a book."

Mr. Khushwant Singh, Indian Writer and Novelist

"You write very well -- indeed, if you weren't such a senior man with Hindustan Lever, I'd be tempted to ask you if you wanted to join the Digest as a writer!"

Mr. Ashok Mahadevan, Editor-In-Chief, Reader's Digest

"I hope you will not let this competitive world crush this talent of yours (writing), and will continue to write."

Mrs. Jaya Bhaduri Bachchan, Movie Star and Member of Indian Parliament

"Your excellent article, I read with interest. I was glad you were a recipient of the Sir Dorabji Tata Trust Special Scholarship for six years, which enabled you to train yourself for a career in business management."

Mr. J.R.D. Tata, Chairman, Tata Sons Limited

"I was touched by your article."

Mrs. Sonia Gandhi, Member of Parliament, President, All India National Congress Party

"I was really touched to read your article in Hindustan Times. Your article gave me great strength to face these trying times with dignity and calmness. My family and myself are grateful to you that you appreciate our services to our Nation and its people."

Mr. Sunil Dutt, Member of Parliament and Minister

"Human Relations in Retail Management is a crucial aspect which is often neglected. Your work is very relevant to India today."

Mr. Nihal Kaviratne CBE, Former Chairman, Unilever Indonesia. Currently Director Glaxo Pharma, India

"Thank you also for enclosing the article that was published in various sections of the media. It made very good reading."

Mr. Amitabh Bachchan, Movie Star and Former Member of Parliament

"I read your article with interest. It deals with the personality and problems of a city. In writing it, you took on a tough assignment. You write very well. The article compares favourably with the writing of professional journalists writing in India."

Mr. Rajinder Puri, Journalist, New Delhi

"It was nice to read your article which you have written and to know that the work of the Missionaries of Charity is so well established in Chandigarh. I am sure they will benefit from your association."

Mr. T. Thomas, Chairman, Hindustan Lever Ltd., and Director, Unilever PLC, London (UK)

"Amazing (Book). A piece of history in itself."

Mr. Nihal Kaviratne CBE, Former Chairman, Unilever Indonesia. Currently Director Glaxo Pharma, India

"I knew you were an interesting and talented writer, but I didn't fully realise how prolific. You seem to have a very clear view of today's and tomorrow's worlds."

Mr. R.D. Morgal, Vice-President, Dale Carnegie & Associates, New York (USA)

"I enjoyed your nostalgic piece in Indian Express. You have a unique knack of looking at places and people, which is the hallmark of a good raconteur. I expect one of these days you will write a magnum opus."

Dr. Ashok Ganguly, Chairman, Hindustan Lever Ltd. and Director, Unilever PLC, London (UK)

"I was happy to read your column on Gandhiji. Wish you the best."

Dr. Sanjaya Baru, Media Advisor, Prime Minister of India

"You have obviously become a considerable authority on the subject of Rural Distribution. I have read with much interest the newspaper articles in which you are quoted."

Mr. P.V.M. Egan, Former Director, Unilever Plc, London

"Rajendra Aneja, has gained international recognition for his role in tapping India's rural markets."

Mr. Salil Tripathi, Asia INC.

"We have officials tell us there is no road here, or this village is there," says Rajendra Aneja. "But from our maps we know there is a road, and that the village is not where they think it is."

"For operations elsewhere, Rural Marketing is a model of how to tap emerging Third World Consumerism: Rajendra Aneja has just been to a conference in Hong Kong to tell sales teams from Southeast Asia and China how it is done."

Mr. Hamish McDonald, Asia's Leading Companies, Far Eastern Economic Review

"I can see; you are the master-mind of Rural Marketing strategy."

Mr. Robert Field, Former Director, Nippon Lever, Japan

"Judging by past experience, it will take three to five years of 'blood and sweat' to get the system running properly and many hurdles await. But Mr. Aneja is convinced that the project (Bicycle Brigade) will vindicate his belief that even with a little innovation even the poorest economies offer a wealth of opportunities."

Mr. Mark Turner, Bicycle Brigade Takes Unilever to The People, Financial Times, UK

"Rajendra Aneja, the brains behind the rural thrust of Hindustan Lever."

The Economic Times

"Executives will be able to plan the routes for the promotional and cinema vans more effectively and to judge the results more easily. As Mr. Rajendra Aneja says: 'We have to combine twentieth century methods with the needs of eighteenth century village life.'"

Mr. Trevor Humphries, Mapping Out Sales to India, Financial Times (UK)

"Your article makes fascinating reading. You have combined the ambitions of Alvin Toffler and Nostradamus into one and expressed it in the terse style of Francis Bacon."

**Mr. Bhau Phansalkar, General Sales Manager,
Hindustan Lever Ltd.**

"I have always enjoyed working with you and admired the progress we have made in Tanzania in recent times and wish you all the best in further building the business."

Dr. Manfred Stach, President Africa, Unilever

"I want to thank you for your dedication, which clearly went beyond the call of duty, to make Unilever once again a prominent player in the economic growth of Tanzania. All that I did to help in the process was only a facilitator duty: without your personal commitment and that of Unilever, nothing much would have come of it.

I also appreciate your contribution in terms of ideas towards creating a better environment for business in our country, and in terms of wide economic reform and growth through the work of the Tanzania National Business Council.

It would have served us well if you had stayed longer with us, but we wish you equally great success in your new assignment in the Ivory Coast."

**His Excellency, President of The United Republic Of
Tanzania, Mr. Benjamin William Mkapa**

"Other multinationals should follow the example of Unilever in Tanzania. The Government recognises your contributions in technology also. You are also promoting capacity utilisation. The government commends and thanks you for that."

His Excellency, Vice President of Tanzania, Dr. Omar Ali Juma

"I am very impressed by the efforts and quality of products."

His Excellency, Prime Minister of Tanzania, Mr. Fredrick Sumaye

"The growth achieved by Unilever Tanzania, is the envy of any company. About my support when you were building your company in Tanzania. I was glad to be associated with what you were doing, and had great admiration for what you achieved."

His Excellency, Former British High Commissioner, Tanzania, Mr. Bruce Dinwiddy

"In some countries, simply distributing products to densely populated urban districts and far-flung rural areas represents a major challenge. Tanzania has 100,000 retail outlets across a country with more than 9,000 villages. Half the population lives below the poverty line and earns less than a dollar a day. Our newly established company set up an innovative 'bicycle brigade' of sales people, drawn from local unemployed young people, to supply small shops with products such as Key laundry soap, sold in small units for a few pence. A year after its launch, its affordability and availability earned it an estimated 10% market share."

Unilever: Social Review

"I very much hope that the situation in Cote d'Ivoire returns to normal which would give you an opportunity to show your full potential in promoting the growth of your company's operation as you did in Tanzania."

His Excellency, High Commissioner of India in Tanzania, Mr. Virendra Gupta

"Thanks for your contributions to our business and organisation. You leave Latin America better for having been with us."

Mr. Charlie Strauss, President, Latin America

"I read your moving tribute to Tanzania....But what moved me even more was the fact, that the talents of such an outstanding businessman, as yourself are no longer available to a country that needs them so badly."

Mr. Michael Holman, Africa Editor, Financial Times, London

"The recent arrival of Unilever has shown that, with the right management, Tanzanians can create top class products."

Mr. Mark Turner, Financial Times, London

"I congratulate you for successfully putting a world class Company on Tanzania's map. It is usually difficult to begin operations in a new country but the manner in which you handled the exercise is commendable."

Mr. Andy Chande, Chairman Barclays Bank, Tanzania And Tanzania Railways Corporation

"Your tenure in Tanzania not only established and nurtured your company's business interests so well in Tanzania, but, even more valuable was your approach to the people here – so friendly and full of warm generosity."

His Excellency, High Commissioner of India to Tanzania, Mr. Dinesh K. Jain

"Indeed it is your effort, which made Unilever to be what it is today in Tanzania."

Mr. Melkizedeck E. Sanare, Commissioner General, Tanzania Revenue Authority, Ministry of Finance

"Bajaj Institute introduced Rural Marketing and Dr. Ghosh asked me to take that class. It was then that we realised that there was lack of published literature on the subject. It was in that context that I came across your articles. I remember having quoted you in my Bajaj lectures. In the company I work for they quote you for their new client pitches and refer to you as a Rural Marketing Specialist. In fact, one of the reasons why I agreed to go to S. P. Jain Institute was to listen to you. Very honestly, I do not think there are many people around with your kind of hands-on experience in Rural Marketing."

Mr. Suren Chawla, Director, Mudra Communications, Bombay

"'Rural Marketing' article. I am indeed proud that a young man who started with us is doing so well."

Mr. E.A. Kshirsagar, Managing Partner, A.F. Ferguson & Co.

"The Business India paper is really good and frankly is very much in agreement with what I believe. I think the points you have made are very worthwhile, indeed. I will try to use them in one of our training sessions for executives. I hope you will continue to write as this is a worthwhile contribution that you are making."

Mr. Tarun Gupta, Former Vice President, Sandoz (I) Ltd.

"I have been a silent appreciator of your writings - for their appeal, quality and your insights of Indian (rural) markets. We offer a course on Rural Marketing, to our post-graduate students. I felt that your speaking to them directly will have several benefits."

Professor D. Nagabrahamam, Director, T.A. Pai Management Institute, Manipal, Karnataka

"I have seen the handwritten manuscript of your Book, 'A challenge to the Nation' today (on the Indo-China war). I have found it very good and useful. From the index of the Book itself I could gauge the book. Your future projects are also interesting and useful."

Mrs. Madalasa Devi Agarwal, Wife of Mr. Shriman Narayan, Former Indian Ambassador to Nepal and former Governor of Gujarat

"An opportunity to find uncommon efforts of a young friend in diverse directions is a rare pleasure indeed. Rajendra Aneja has a philosophy, which may today be very vague, even ridiculous in the eyes of a non-believing few. But it contains seeds of a splendid plant, which may bear a rare variety of fruits if properly nursed and watered. I pray to god to create such circumstances as may help this process in his own generosity."

To R.K.A. my request is 'Do your best and leave the rest to God', be his humble tool."

Mr. Bachhraj Vyas, Former President, Jan Sangh
(now the Bharatiya Janata Party)

"Shri Rajendra Aneja was awarded the Rotary Trophy for being the Best Student of the College. A first class student, he has well defined views on education, on the students' role in the developing economy and on student discipline. The speech that he made after the Rotary Trophy was awarded to him is ample testimony to the sincerity and fervour with which he holds his views. It is difficult to come across such a boy with a rare combination of sense of duty and dedication, idealism and urge for social service."

Editorial, Sydenham College Magazine

"I have great pleasure in saying that I have known Shri Rajendra Aneja since June 1967 when he joined the Sydenham College as a freshman. I happen to know Rajendra intimately and at close quarters since he was entrusted to my care and supervision as a Sir Dorab Tata Scholar throughout his stay at this college.

Shri Aneja speaks English fluently and writes it with precision, correctness and force. His letters to the newspaper are marked by sane logic, sound common sense and vigorous expression. Shri Aneja is a young man of great intellectual integrity, sound values and rare sense of dedication to the job in hand."

Professor K.R. Maheshi, Head of the English Department, Sydenham College of Commerce and Economics

"Finally got a chance to read your brilliant, and well written post. I was thinking that if the USA was lucky you might write a book about or for us. Totally agreed with your summary, 'Ultimately corporations must serve the societal goals of providing quality goods, generating surpluses for investment, creating employment, contributing to the environment and development. If they do not, then, they are better dead, than to survive as financial and societal parasites.'

Once again, thanks for your interesting, informative, and insightful post."

Lou from Queens (USA), Financial Times UK

"We must also mention people like Rajendra K. Aneja (Dubai), who write regularly or at frequent intervals to enliven our pages with letters that are 'short and coming from the heart', to quote Kenneth Gregory who edited the collection of letters to the London Times."

A.M. Pakkar Koya, Senior Editor, Arab News

"Normally people read the front page, but since Mr. Rajendra Aneja started writing letters, I always open the letters page first. He is a sea of knowledge. You should learn from him."

Reader, Letters to Editor, 7 Days, UAE

"Mr. Rajendra Aneja's opinions on various subjects are praiseworthy, it seems he has travelled a lot and his writings reflect his in-depth knowledge on the issues."

Reader, Letters to Editor, 7 Days UAE

"It appears that Rajendra Aneja is a phantom figure created to support 7 Days propaganda enacted by someone else, to provoke readers' reactions.

If he is what your paper portrays, it would clear doubts if his photograph appeared in your paper, so that we as readers can find out for ourselves, as the saying goes," A picture is worth a thousand words." Surely an intellectual with the self-confidence of Mr. Rajendra Aneja would consent."

A Reader in 7 Days

"We assure that Mr. Aneja is no phantom figure. However, it is not 7 Days place to "out" its letter writers."

Editor, 7 Days

"How true that is what Rajendra K Aneja wrote on 15th August! And it makes so much practical sense."

A Reader in Dubai

"I am a big fan of RKA. Dear RKA, you are doing great guns. Keep that going."

A Reader in Dubai

"It was interesting to read Rajendra Aneja's brilliant letter to the Editor. Was there healthy cynicism inside there? Of course, there will be, and the records as wonderfully stated by Mr. Aneja speak for themselves. Evidently a well-researched letter for the facts were 100 per cent correct. It's a nice feeling to be an Indian, the warts and blemishes as so correctly pinpointed by Mr. Aneja notwithstanding!"

A Reader in Dubai

"I admire Rajendra for his courage and just assessment of world affairs, it seems like most people have forgotten 9/11 and how dangerous the world would have been if it hadn't been for the war on terror."

Reader in Dubai

"Though I do not know him personally, my understanding is that Mr. Rajendra Aneja's opinions on various subjects are praise worthy, it seems he has travelled a lot and his writings reflects his in depth knowledge on the issues."

A Reader in Dubai

"I found Mr. Aneja's letters like a candle light brought into a house of darkness."

Reader, Letters to Editor, Gulf Daily News, Bahrain

Contents

Sr. No.	Subject	Page No.

Sr. No.	Subject	Page No.

Sr. No.	Subject	Page No.

Sr. No.	Subject	Page No.

5. Anatomy Of Leadership — 139

Sr. No.	Subject	Page No.

7. Universal Value Of A Salesman — 168

Sr. No.	Subject	Page No.

9. Revolution In Global Rural Market — 221

Sr. No.	Subject	Page No.

Sr. No.	Subject	Page No.

Sr. No.	Subject	Page No.

Sr. No.	Subject	Page No.

19. Art Of Attending Training Courses — 311

Sr. No.	Subject	Page No.

20. Productive Business Travel — 321

* * *

The Customer is always right. This is an axiom in business. No algorithm can change it. Never, ever fight with a Customer.

* * *

1

Prologue

1.   Customer Is Always Right

The Customer is always right. This is an axiom in business. No algorithm can change it. Never, ever fight with a Customer.

2.   Marketing Failure Is Impossible

Markets have multiple layers of segments, incomes, tastes and preferences. So every product can find a segment or layer of demand. It is impossible for any product to fail, if you are determined to succeed. There is always a market for any product you launch, somewhere in the world. The skill lies in discovering the markets and servicing them effectively.

3.   Study Basic Human Needs

Study basic human needs and aspiration to design new businesses or products. Mark Zuckerberg identified the basic human need to connect and make friends and launched Facebook. Jeffrey Bezos learnt that consumers want a wide range, lowest prices and quick home delivery. He launched Amazon. Both these entrepreneurs have become legends.

4.   Family Members Are Customers

Your family members and friends are also customers. Think of them, when you construct new products or services.

5.   Marketing: Analysis, Not Glamour

Marketing is very solemn, hard analysis and work. You have to architect a product, which people will want to buy. Do not let the glamour, music, lights and models dazzle or enamour you.

6.   Plan, Plan, Plan

Successful managers plan. They have a five-year plan, an annual plan and a monthly plan for the company.

7.   Learn to Read the Shops

A market visit, to meet grocers, wholesalers and supermarket staff, is not merely an opportunity to shake hands. An astute manager learns to read, repeat read, shops and supermarkets. Through sheer observation, a smart manager can estimate market shares by studying shops in the market.

8. Breathe, Dream Sales Targets

The sales team must breathe and dream of their targets, round the clock. We printed a Sales Target Card, measuring three inches by four inches, wrote the name of each salesperson and his brand targets on it. We told the field force to carry it in their pockets all the time. In the night they were told to keep it under their pillows. If they achieved their targets they were rewarded with gold or stock options. Everyone met his target. After 30 years, when these salespersons meet me, they say those stocks are their old-age insurance covers.

9. Value Institutional Customers

A smart company will service and harvest army canteens (grocery outlets for the army), police co-operative societies, hotels of all-star categories, restaurants, hospitals, prisons, etc. All these institutions are huge customers, who need products of all types. Cater to them for incremental sales.

10. Tough Times: Sell More

Businesses can go through tough times. Then it may be difficult to meet the bottom-line. Put gargantuan, monolithic, monstrous efforts to increase sales and market shares. Let every employee in the company beat the streets to sell more. It can be done.

11. Explore Greenfields

If sales just do not grow, explore Greenfields. Go to hitherto unexplored territories, market countries. If the urban areas do not deliver, tap the rural markets and slums. If a country does not deliver, tap surrounding countries. Never stop exploring.

12. Harvest War-Torn Countries

Always service war impacted countries. They are dangerous and difficult to service. Every company is running away from them. You just hang on. Find some wholesalers to service the markets in war-torn areas in Iraq, Syria, Yemen, etc. Feed these wholesalers, who will reach the products to the people. Even when there is a war, people need to eat, drink and wash clothes.

13. Accounts, Crystal Clear

Always keep the accounts of the company, crystal clear like a bowl of clean water.

14. Accounting Conservativeness

Always provide judiciously for exigencies, emergencies and cost overruns. Avoid over-optimistic scenarios. In accounting, it is better to be safe, than sorry.

15.   Margins by Brand and Store

Review margins by brand and pack every month. In a Retail Business, every Store must generate profits. If some brands, packs or stores are not contributing profits, prepare turnaround plans for them to do so, with time targets. If they yet do not deliver, chop them. Every brand, pack and store must generate profits. There can be no dawdlers.

16.   Cash in the Wallet

Despite the credit cards, cash in the wallet, provides comfort and power to every person. Similarly, ensure that the company is always cash rich.

17.   Money Must Not Rest or Idle

Money should never be left to rest or idle, by an individual or a company. Money must grow round-the-clock. So if you have surplus cash, invest it in stocks, deposits, gold, real estate, etc.

18.   Deep-Drill Every Cost

Every cent matters in a Business. So drill deep into every cost. Whether it is the total raw material cost or the office cleaning expenses, review them rigorously, to get the best price. The lowest cost is not always the best price. Price should be related to the quality of service being provided.

19. Key Performance Parameter

Every business has a key performance parameter, which is the key to the entire financial story. Mr. M.S. Oberoi, Chairman of one of the largest and respected global hotel chains, wanted to know the aggregate occupancy rate of the hotel chain, every evening. He could project the entire financial picture through this one digit. Identify one or a maximum of three such parameters, which provide clues to the entire business for the day.

20. Daily, One-Page Financial Summary

The Finance department should furnish a One-Page Financial Summary for the CEO every morning, providing important details of the previous day and cumulative year on sales, cash flows, outstanding, working capital, etc.

21. Chairman and Financial Figures

If you are a CEO or Chairman, with a non-financial background like marketing or production, make sure you fall in love with figures. Learn to read a profit and loss statement and a balance sheet, backwards. Go to a private tutor if you have to, burn the midnight oil alone at home. However, make sure you waltz with financial figures better than any accountant.

22.   Frugality Is Wise

Frugality saves money. It also generates an environment of cost-effectiveness. The Chairman of Hindustan Lever Ltd., always travelled in an indigenously manufactured Ambassador car, when the only option was imported cars, to signal frugality in the enterprise.

23.   Commodities: Figures plus Fields

If you are in the commodity business, you will be inundated with market data from a dozen screens, throughout the day and night. Great. Study the information and process it. However do not forget the markets and fields. Travel to the "mandis" (wholesale markets) and fields to understand what is happening to the crops. One of my finest bosses, Mr. B.R. Shah, Buying Director of Hindustan Lever Ltd, could travel in the Gujarat state in India and opine authoritatively about the next year's groundnut crop output, by just observing the plants and the flowers, in the fields along the roads.

24.   Dangers of Borrowed Funds

Never borrow to spend on daily expenses. Manage that through internal accruals. Borrow to expand, diversify and invest in expansion. Smart companies invest in new projects also through internal accruals, so that they save on debt-servicing costs. The right balance in leveraging is critical for the financial health of the enterprise. Overleveraging led to the catastrophic 2008 global financial crisis, which plunged the world into misery.

25. Respect Your Vendors

Never take advantage of your vendors by squeezing them, even if you can do so, by virtue of the size and reputation of the business. The vendors will work with the business under pressure, but will always be looking for an exit. That business is fair, where everybody benefits.

26. Nerves – Information Technology

Information is the new bloodline of any business, just like the blood that flows through the nerves of the human body. There cannot be any stoppage or block, even for a second. So chose the best IT systems, hardware and software for the business.

27. IT and Customers

Management Information Technology and Systems are the new heartbeat of any business. It tells you what is happening in the business and where. However, listen to the other heartbeat also, customers.

28. Automate the Production

Get the best possible production machinery, automate it and update as often as possible. Reduce production costs and process losses to the lowest levels.

29. Production Planning

Always produce as per the demand forecast, not as per the inventories of war materials in the warehouse or a gut feel.

30. Stop the Production Line

If you are senior and strong enough and see something wrong with the product being produced, have the courage to stop the production and initiate corrective action. Do not let a shoddy product leave the factory gate. Your stopping the product line will send a shudder down the spine of the company. The message will be loud and clear: Quality is paramount.

31. Human Relations: Born to Serve

The primary task of the Human Relations (HR) function is to serve all the other functions of the organisation. HR is a service function.

32. Look After the People

Look after the people who manage the business; then they will look after the business and also you. On my confirmation contact in 1976 in the market, I was hit by a car and flew about 10 feet in the air like a football. Mercifully I survived and landed on my feet. Mr. Bipin Shah, the Head of the Foods Business at Hindustan Lever, who was assessing me, immediately took me to a clinic and then to a top orthopaedic and got me thoroughly checked for any internal or external injury. Then, he brought me to my house in his own car and spent an hour with my Father, reassuring him, that I was fine. I pay my respects to him whenever I meet him, even now, four decades later.

33. Never Short-Change Anybody

No company should ever short-change anybody. They will find out sooner or later. Then they will want to get their own back.

34. Always, Always, Have One Boss

The best of careers get messed up, when too many people try to boss over a person or an operation. Let every manager or director, have just one boss to report to. Too many cooks always spoil the broth.

35. Believe in Your Selection System

A bright student failed the MBA exam, much to his own and everyone's surprise. However, he had already been selected and had joined one of the largest multinational corporations. This multinational had an unwritten rule, if you failed your MBA exam, you had to go. The issue went to the Chairman of the company. He said, "We have more faith, in our selection system, than the evaluation system of an MBA Programme." My friend kept his job and is a captain of industry today.

36. Have Blue-Sky Days

Have a Blue-Sky day every year. Take your core team, to a mountain or sea resort for one or two days every year and talk to them freely. Are we moving in the right direction? How can we buoy the company further? What more can we do? What are the employees feeling? What do customers expect?

37. Shake Hands Joyfully

If you have to shake hand with an employee, who has to leave, send him out with a smile. Do not play around with his dues or pensions. Be a specialist in generating smiles.

38. Respect Retired Staff, Ex-employees

People who have worked in the company in the past have contributed to it. They may have retired or left. People who have served the company should be treated with respect. Have a cup of tea with them annually.

* * *

Capturing Global Emerging Consumers is tough.

"In the end you are exhausted in mind, body and spirit. Only one thing keeps you going, a vision, a dream you once had."

- Paul Nurmi, Olympic Gold medallist.

* * *

2

Winning Global Customers

Our New World

39. World of Choices

Our era is characterised by the large number of choices available to customers across the world. Whether a consumer is buying a soap or a refrigerator, a razor blade or a car, a packet of butter or a computer, a consumer has multiple choices available in the retail shops, hypermarkets or e-commerce platforms, irrespective of whether he or she lives in Myanmar, Vietnam, China, India, Botswana, Congo, Russia, Poland, USA or Alaska.

40. Borderless World

The world is gradually becoming borderless. Thus, there is international competition in almost all products with sellers vying with each other, to have a share of the consumers' wallet. True, there are periodic tariff wars. Nevertheless products flow across countries more easily now, than ever in the past.

41. Life Is All About Selling

Guess who said, "We are going to sell Jack, like soapflakes!" The father of President John Kennedy, when the family decided to field the young aspirant for the top job in the USA. The fact is that even Presidents of countries have to be sold and marketed.

42. President Obama's Victory

President Obama's brilliant and aggressive campaign in 2008, constituted a brilliant marketing and sales management case study.

43. New Middle Class

Across the world, a billion people will join the middle class shortly. In Russia, 78 per cent of people, are classified as middle class. Moreover, the middle class like to buy. And buy.

44. Asia and Africa

In the next few decades, the maximum growth will be in Asia and Africa. Consumers in emerging markets will get richer faster and will be prime global spenders.

Emerging Global Consumers

45. Business and People

Eventually, business is all about People, across the globe.

46. New Consumers and Innovations

There is need for innovations to meet the needs of consumers who are entering the monetary economy for the first time. Corporations need to understand how these new consumers, adopt products and the role of branding.

47. Slums: Two Billion Consumers

About one to two billion people live in slums across the world, though concentrated in Africa, Latin America and Asia. They are organised communities with their own social norms and codes. They too have aspirations of moving out of slums. Many will. Companies have to devise mechanisms to work with the local inhabitants.

48. New Paradigms

Women, youth, rural markets, slums, middle classes are large segments. Corporations are soul-searching: How well are we squeezing each segment, each piece of the pyramid?

49. Villages, Value for Money

The living conditions of three billion global people in the villages, are improving due to augmenting agricultural productivity. Villagers are more open to experimenting with brands. However, they will buy value for money brands.

50. Major Changes in Lives

There are major changes taking place in the lives of the 85 per cent of the world that is broadly classified as middle class and poor in the global economy. They are more open to experimenting with brands, in their desire to improve their quality of life. The mobile phone has given immense power to farmers in Brazil, India and China to keep tab on prices in regional markets.

51. Emerging Consumers: New Young

The world is becoming a younger place. About 42 per cent of the world is below the age of 24 years. For this generation, "Internet is a birth right!" This is a new breed with a new creed. It requires quick and instant fixes. This generation believes in "Me, mine, and myself!" It has no memories of World War II, or of famines, or Great Depressions. The laptop, internet and mobile phone have shrunk the world for this generation. Are corporations ready for meeting the needs of this new generation?

52. Women: Emerging Consumers

Affluent women are the single largest growing force, in the global economy. The private wealth of women adds up to USD 39.6 trillion globally (roughly the same size of Asia-Pacific regions' USD 37 trillion in combined wealth), according to Boston Consulting Group. Of the women whose private net worth was over USD 100,000, 44 per cent were self-made as entrepreneurs or company employees. Just 60 women have a total net-worth of USD 53 billion.

53. Emerging Consumer, Incomes

Managing the Emerging Global Consumers can be a tough challenge, when the daily income of the customer is only US cents 35, and even a toothbrush costs USD two, in many countries in Africa like Kenya and Tanzania.

54. New Entrants to Monetary Economy

Many customers in Emerging segments are frequently just entering the monetary economy. In the deep interiors of the tribal forests of India, salt is yet used as the medium of exchange and barter is practiced. Therefore, these consumers generally have limited moneys.

55. Data Issues

Reliable hard data pertaining to Emerging Global Consumer categories is not easy to access. It can also be unreliable.

56. Fickle Brand Loyalties

New consumers are open to experimenting and can be fickle in brand loyalties. They are volatile in their preferences. They are constantly transiting income levels in their ambition to improve their lot and are hence fluid in their tastes and loyalties.

57. Rural Opinion Leaders

Local opinion leaders like the village school teacher, priest, doctor, etc., also influence rural consumers. Word of mouth and local recommendations, contribute significantly to brand acceptance in the villages.

58. Impact of Television

Television has made economically weak people more politically aware of their own rights as citizens. They respect the educated members of their community i.e. a doctor, an engineer, a professor, etc. Moreover, Hollywood and Bollywood movies influence their fashion and daily lives.

59. Rural TV Advertising

The use of same TV commercial for the urban areas and the rural areas, is frequently a mistake.

60. Where Do People Buy?

About 26 per cent of the world's consumers yet buy their foods and daily necessities from small groceries and shops. Again, about 50 per cent of the global population, shops at hypermarkets and supermarkets. E-commerce is the new channel capturing hearts and wallets across the world.

61. Logistics, Information Technology

The crucial criterion: Is the brand travelling down to the supermarket, shopkeeper and the Emerging Global Consumer across the world? Logistics and Information Technology have become integral with the customer-management function.

62. Understand Shopkeeper Mindset

Corporations need to understand the mind-set and operations of ordinary grocers. How?

a) Observe shopkeepers in their shops,
b) Study their shelves and the range of products,
c) Understand their inventory management,
d) Study their customers and flow of store traffic,
e) Send management trainees, to work in shops ("deep-dive") for about one to three months, to comprehend retail operations.

63. Retailers in Emerging Economies

a) Retailers are family or proprietary firms,
b) They select products based on reputation of company or the influence of the salesperson,
c) Retailers allocate space to brands, based on the salesperson's relationship,
d) Family members are involved in managing the business,
e) The daily cash generation is the basis of the business, not the monthly profitability.

64. Aspirations of Women

In many countries like Kenya, Nigeria and Myanmar, women also run wholesale outlets. Some even become distributors of companies. Women are taking to retailing and trading to supplement the household incomes. Many women commence businesses to fulfil their own instincts and aspirations of being bright businesswomen.

65. Distribution Elements

A major challenge in selling to Emerging Global Consumer markets, is to get the product to the shop and to the consumer. There are five key elements in the distribution chain i.e. the Company Distributor, Urban Wholesalers, Rural Wholesalers, Rural Sub-stockist and the Shopkeepers.

66. Simple Distribution Goal

The goal is simple, to feed the smallest of retailers. Sometimes these marginal outlets are small and many may have an aggregate inventory of only USD 100 in the outlet. These outlets also, have to be serviced regularly.

67. Reach the Customer, Anyhow

Is the brand travelling down the line? The company may have to use a donkey, a horse-cart, a handcart or a mechanised vehicle. The stocks must reach the shopkeeper and the consumer.

68. Managing the Field Force

The major critical catalyst, in tapping Emerging Consumers is the salesperson. He has a critical and tough job. His assignment is lonely. He works in remote markets, where the infrastructure of accommodation and transportation is fragile. Sometimes, it is difficult to even get a meal.

69. Cost of Servicing

The cost of serving an outlet in the villages in the developing countries, where many Emerging Consumers live, can be twice or even thrice, that of servicing an urban outlet, due to distances and the dispersion of shops.

70.   Fluid Markets

Global players need to be present in most segments of the markets. Products, markets and media are now fluid. They flow across geographical boundaries and across income categories. Every company has consumers from slums to the super-rich. Long-term survival and success will depend on tapping the potential of all the segments.

71.   Marginal Inputs, Bountiful Rewards

In the Emerging Global Consumers markets, marginal focus, inputs and endeavours, can yield bountiful rewards.

72.   Impulsive Consumers

How do companies deal with, mercurial customers who ceaselessly flirt with new brands? Quite simply, companies, have to be nimble footed and learn to dance the samba, salsa or merengue, as the customer desires.

73.   Seed Products in Villages

Corporations would be smart to seed their brands in the rural markets. The living conditions of the rural poor, are improving. The earlier a company taps this massive emerging segment, the more embedded its brand names will be, in consumer minds and psyches.

74. Little Focus, Big Dividends

The products of most global corporations travel down to the smallest of shops through the wholesaler network. So, even a little focus by the companies can yield overwhelming dividends.

75. Some Countries: Turmoil

Tapping Emerging Global Consumer markets rigorously, may require muscles of iron. Many markets, in Africa and Asia are vessels of turmoil, political upheavals, rebellions, etc. When politics reigns supreme, global companies just have to put their heads down and adhere tightly to the script.

76. Impediments, Emerging Markets

Tapping Emerging Global Consumer markets is not exactly a bed of roses. It is tough, sustainable work. It is a demanding assignment, for the infrastructure is fragile. Purchasing power is growing, but it is yet circumscribed. Whilst education and media percolation have broadened perspectives, traditional attitudes are not easy to change. Marketing mixes have to be fine-tuned for the target audiences.

77. Making Brands Dance

The key goal is to make brands dance and generate profits in the Emerging Global Consumer segments. For this it is necessary to recognise that:

a) Brand Building

Brands are built by the efforts of marketing and sales thrusts. Brand building is a multifunctional process. It requires synergy and consistent effort.

b) Servicing Trade

Supermarkets account for about 50 per cent of global sales. However in the developing world, small groceries play an important role. Thus an enterprise has to judiciously serve the Modern Trade and the traditional small stores.

c) Arm's Reach Availability

Coke's philosophy is to put their products "within arm's reach of desire" anywhere in the world. Products must be accessible constantly to customers.

d) Ethical Practices

The trade respects companies with ethical practices. Company should build trade goodwill, with good professional practices.

e) Merchandising Sways

About 75 per cent of the world yet shops at grocery stores and supermarkets. Hence merchandising and point of sales, can sway sales.

78. Five Lessons, Emerging Consumers

The five key success factors in harvesting Emerging Global Consumer markets are (1) Evolving Markets, (2) Continuous Growth, (3) Develop Local Talent, (4) Brand Margins, and (5) Designing Local Products.

79. Evolving Markets

Markets are constantly evolving due to more consumers entering the monetary economy and changes in fashion. So consumers and markets should be studied ceaselessly and strategic and operational plans should incorporate consumer preferences.

80. Continuous Growth

An enterprise should grow continuously. It can grow through organic growth and also through strategic local acquisitions. Both these can improve market penetration and shares.

81. Develop Local Talent

Develop local cadres of managers and operators to harvest the markets. Local staff costs less, knows the culture of the market and how the land lies. Sometimes, intensive training has to be imparted to upgrade skills.

82. Brands Margins

Ensure that brands make margins from day one, since this helps to focus on generating sales.

83. Designing Local Products

To architecture products for local markets, it is best to study consumers intensively and then take the best of global and local research to craft products that will get acceptance rapidly.

84. Time Consuming Process

Tapping Emerging Global Consumer markets is an exacting and a time-consuming process. As the great American poet, Robert Frost, wrote, "The woods are lovely, dark and deep; but I have miles to go before I sleep, I have miles to go before I sleep." And, you fight on. Losing is not an option. Ever.

Lessons from Latin America

85. Spirit of Latin America

"Even if Mother Nature is against us, we will defy and defeat her!"

- Simon Bolivar, Venezuelan freedom fighter, in the struggle for freedom from the Spanish Empire. (1783-1830).

86. Brazil Is Booming

Brazil's economy is booming. Brazil is big and gigantic. Whether it is a car plant, or the Iguassu Falls or transport trucks or factories or offices, Brazilians like big, huge sizes. They have excellent factories of electronics and plants manufacturing cars, computers, electronics and televisions for Latin America. The country is on an economic roll.

87. Racial Integration

Brazil has integrated people of different racial backgrounds, so beautifully in music, football and even in business. It is a wonderful mosaic.

88. Role of Passion

The Brazilians are fond of music, football and dance. There is passion in that country, among the people to win, to achieve. Passion is also great fun, because it is pretty intoxicating. This passion is also reflected in how they do business.

89. Carnival's Brand Lessons

The Brazilian Carnival taught me, what moves Latino consumers. A brand has to be bright, cheerful and musical to win loyalty among from Latinos. Most brands succeed if they deliver the promise, i.e. the value proposition. However, if the brand can make the usage fun and invigorating, then it is guaranteed to blossom in Latin America.

90. Disparities and Poverty

The prevalence of high disparities in developing countries normally indicates widespread poverty amongst lower income sections of the population.

91. Heart and Soul

The distribution system is the heart and soul of a mass-market products launch, anywhere in the world.

92. Servicing the Poor

Most global corporations have focused efforts to tap the top end of the markets in Latin America. They are frail in servicing villagers and slum dwellers. It is a major challenge to evolve products for those who live on less than USD two per day, i.e. below the poverty line.

93. The Two Brazils

When you think of Brazil, you immediately think of the carnival, football and great beer. However, there is another Brazil, which you see, if you work in the slums. In one of these "favelas" (slums), I met a lady named Maria. Maria lives alone. She burns wood to make charcoal, which she sells for a living. "I earn about two US dollars daily," she tells me. Her children had abandoned her. She could only afford one meal a day. When I asked her what she did when she felt hungry in the night, she replied, "We sleep to forget our hunger". The painful eyes of tired Maria, aged 65, struggling through life, left a deep impression on me.

Later even when I encountered icons like Faustao Silva of Globo TV (Domingão do Faustão), Carolina Gómez Correa (Bogotá) who was Miss Colombia and Miss Universe (First runner-up), Valéria Melo Péris, Miss Brazil, my heart and soul continued to be tormented by Maria's hunger and hurt eyes.

94. Understand the Consumers

The first prerequisite of catering to a new market in the economy segment, is to understand the consumers and their needs. It is educative to spend some months visiting consumers in slums and rural markets, to talk to them about the products they use and their expectations. We would just knock on the doors of homes in shanties and seek the opinions of the homemaker about products that the family uses.

95. A Clean Latin America

Latinos are fastidious about hygiene and cleanliness. Residents of slums and villages were poor, but invariably they kept their homes, roads and pathways spotlessly clean. Laerco Cardoso, my Brazilian colleague summed up, "Our people tell us, 'we may be poor, but we are clean.'"

96. Talk to Consumers

Marketers rely on research or published data, to understand consumers. Eventually, there is no substitute for simply walking the streets, visiting shops in towns, villages and slums to talk to users of products to understand their buying behaviour.

97. Social Laundry

Laundry is a community social activity, in many countries. A mundane chore becomes a social activity. Women meet in groups to chat and wash clothes.

98. Homemaker Contribution

In many lower income categories, the homemaker finds fulfilment, in actually washing the clothes of the family. The more she scrubs the clothes, the more she feels she is contributing to the family.

99. Expose All Managers to Reality

Companies frequently expose only the sales and marketing teams to consumer markets. Accounting, financial and IT professionals also benefit by exposure to consumer realities. They too need to understand consumers and markets.

100. MBAs and Slums

Most corporations recruit MBAs from prestigious institutions. Typically, the recruits hail from middle-class to wealthy families. For many fresh professionals, straight out of university, it is challenging to deal with consumers in villages and slums. The daily remuneration of these professionals would constitute the monthly budget of a slum dwelling family.

101. Deep Dive Immersions

"Immersing" young professionals in the real lives of the consumers, was a brilliant program first initiated in the 1970s, by Mr. T. Thomas, a former Chairman of Hindustan Lever Ltd. Fresh management trainees from business schools lived with rural families in Etah district, in Uttar Pradesh. The trainees had to execute a local project e.g. build a road, dig a well, etc., with the help of the villagers. This helped the fresh graduates to learn about how villagers live and work.

102. Identify Consumer Need

"Identifying a consumer need is the seed of any successful business," opined our Professor John Quelch, at Harvard Business School, at a Training Programme I was attending.

103. Product Must Deliver

Many products, make tall claims, but fail to deliver promises. Eventually, such products lose consumer respect and loyalty.

104. Perfume Is Important

"Have you noticed how Latino customers buy toilet soaps?" asked Frank Schott, the marketing director of Colombia, when I was working in the market with him, in Bogota, Colombia. "The way Indians and Asians do – they pick up a tablet and smell it, through the wrapper!" I responded.

105. New Products, Be Bold

It is not necessary to follow the lead brands in colour or design, when launching new brands. Be bold and take the road not taken.

106. Earning and Spending

A good company, like a smart individual, will always spend less than it earns. And, it will always save some moneys for rainy days and years.

107. Mass-Market Brand's Impact

It is my experience across countries, that a mass-market brand priced 40 to 50 per cent below the lead brand, has absolutely no impact on the lead brand's market share.

108. Hypermarkets: A Social Experience

Emerging consumers love visiting hypermarkets for the air-conditioned and elegant experience. A visit to a top hypermarket over the weekend becomes a social outing in Latin America, Asia and even the Middle East.

109. Distribution in Latin America

Very few companies in Latin America, especially the multinationals, have invested time and effort in building their own exclusive distribution systems, comprising of an exclusive band of distributors servicing small shops.

110. Martins: The King Wholesaler

One of the largest wholesalers I met in Brazil was Martins, a six-decade-old institution. They sell over 10,000 items (SKUs). They service any order across the country within 24 hours of receiving it, through a fleet of over 2,000 delivery trucks. Mr. Martins started his business delivering stocks to small shopkeepers, riding on his own bicycle. Now, he services the entire country.

111. Service Hypermarkets Too

Whilst launching mass-market products, it is debated heatedly whether the organised trade should be serviced simultaneously with the new products. Definitely, yes.

112. Respect the Hospitality

In Piura (Peru), I took repeated gulps of "Cusqueña" beer at eleven in the morning in the market, from a series of large bottles that a retailer insisted on passing around. I just had to shut my mind to the punctiliousness of drinking beer in the market whilst working. "Keep drinking," advised Pepe the sales director of Peru with a wink, "It's a business obligation!"

Wholesalers and retailers are sentimental and take umbrage if you refuse their hospitality, be it a beer or a cup of strong black, bitter coffee. Just drink it. And, enjoy it too.

113. Fearing the Slum Lords

Many companies are petrified of servicing the slums due to possible violence and thefts of stocks and cash. They frequently abandon slum-servicing to wholesalers. However, once the slumlords realise that your only agenda is to sell some consumer products, they leave you alone. If you are lucky, you may even be offered a bottle of the splendid Brazilian "Brahma" beer.

114. Conquer the Amazona River

No company had hitherto dreamt of tapping the villages along the banks of the 6,400 kilometres long River Amazona. We had dared. However, we had merely scratched the surface. Every country has markets on the banks of their rivers, waiting to be harvested.

115. Dress like a Girl to Work

As a tribute to the women of Brazil, on Fridays, in certain parts of the country, it is the done thing to dress up like a girl. In Salvador, we were launching one of our key brands. Some of my local sales colleagues, would dress up like girls on Friday! That means dresses, lipstick, perfumes, eye shadows and eyelashes. Then they went to the market to work. No one was surprised, because even a few shopkeepers are also dressed like girls. This is a compliment to girls!

116. Resonance with Consumers

In advertising brands, it is important to select themes, platforms, models and scenarios, which resonate with the target consumers.

117. Tell a Story

We all know, how important it is to be able to tell a story. The four words, "Once upon a time…" are ingrained in our childhood psyches, by the stories our grandparents and parents told us, as kids. The best advertising will always tell a story. People love stories. Steve Jobs began his major presentations by saying, "Today, I want to tell you three stories from my life. That's it. No big deal. Just three stories."

Alex Haley once counselled that the best way to begin a speech is "Let me tell you a story."

118. Pillars of Product Launch

Merchandising and displays should be the robust pillars of any product launch.

119. Merchandising Mania

In the classic movie, "Citizen Kane", Charles Kane (Orson Welles), advises his reporters, "If the headline is big, the news becomes big!"

I have learnt that if the displays of a new brand are gigantic in the shops, the brand becomes giant news!

120. Size Matters

When the movie Titanic, won the Oscar, the Director, James Cameron, exulted, about the long ship and the movie, which was 3 hours and 14 minutes, "Sometimes, size does matter".

Well it does, in wall paintings, too. The bigger and longer the wall painting is, the greater is the impact.

121. Football, a Religion

Football is a sacred religion in all Latino countries. Hence, sponsorship of local football matches with the product's brand name can enable soaring awareness.

122. Frugality Is Wise

In launching economy priced, mass consumption products, every element of the costs should be identified and pruned, to ensure cost effectiveness. Margins are low in the initial stages, due to advertising and promotion expenses. Hence, frugality and prudence are wise.

123. Music Mesmerises

Music mesmerises Latinos. Thus, product commercials should always be interspersed with locally appealing "samba" music in Brazil.

124. Missing a Hero, Gabriel Marquis

That night I returned from Cartagena to Charleston Hotel, in Bogotá. I remonstrated to my friend Beth at the reception, how I had missed meeting Gabriel Garcia Marquis, the Nobel Prize winning Colombian writer, at his house, in Cartagena. "Why did you not tell me that you wanted to meet him?" she screamed. "He has been staying here for many weeks. Perhaps you crossed him in the lobby or breakfasted at the "La Biblioteca" restaurant with him many times, without knowing it!" she explicated. I could hear my heart crack.

An African Corporate Safari

125. The Customer Is Divine

Turning a customer away is like turning God away from your home, in any market in the world.

126. Dreams, Visions

A company without dreams and a vision, is a person without a soul. Dreams inspire people and spur them to huge achievements. Dreams also prevent despondencies when everything goes wrong!

127. Five Building Blocks

To achieve a breakthrough in market leadership, a company needs to focus on five key Building Blocks, i.e.:

1) Customer-Service,
2) Building Brand Equities,
3) Strong Corporate Affairs,
4) Commercial Controls,
5) Local Production.

128. Success and Passion

Success must become an all-consuming passion.

129. Mexico Olympics, 1968

"Out of the darkness he entered the stadium – his leg bloody and bandaged. John Stephen Akhwari of Tanzania was hobbling with pain. An hour earlier, the packed stadium had seen the Marathon winner finish. As Akhwari crossed the finish line, the small crowd stood to its feet, cheering with admiration. Later a reporter asked the runner why he had not just given up, as he had no chance of winning. He answered, "My country did not send me to Mexico Olympics to start the race. They sent me to finish."

130. Have a Dream

A strong dream can defeat many deprivations.

131. Your Own Path

"Nothing is written"

- T.E. Lawrence of Arabia

132. Business Strategy in One Line

Brilliant Professor David Yoffie, of Harvard Business School, taught us to write the Business strategy of any company, however large, in one simple sentence. This forces you to think, think and think.

133. Values and Precedents

When you are new in any country, the government, media, consumers and even employees watch you closely. As George Washington, a former US President (1789–1797) once stated, we have to establish precedents. Moreover, a new company has to ensure that the precedents are based on values.

134. Building Enterprise Culture

Enterprise culture can be cemented if we:

a) Invest seriously in training and development of staff,
b) Give staff an opportunity to diversify skills and grow,
c) Promote from within, whenever possible,
d) Encourage objectivity and transparency,
e) Maintain a fine balance between expatriates and local staff.

135. Integrity in Business

Integrity has to be all-pervasive in the operations of a company. Write it in stone. Hard it may be, but try to walk on water. On the fundamentals, break, rather than bend.

136. Vision and Courage

If you have the vision and courage, there are no limits to growth. The only limitation to achievement is one's own vision.

137. Vision to Digits

What does the word "Vision", mean? A dream must have a deadline, to become a vision. A vision must be reduced to digits, to become a reality. Otherwise, visions are nothing but colourful kites in the skies. A vision or a mission that is not reduced to digits by the operating personnel is a fairy tale.

138. Vision Is Work

A Vision is only one per cent dream, nine per cent deadlines and planning and 90 per cent diligence.

139. Have a Dream

If you do not have much money or reserves, have a dream. Anyone who has a dream is not poor.

140. Weariness and Vision

"In the end you are exhausted in mind, body and spirit. Only one thing keeps you going, a vision, a dream you once had."

- Paul Nurmi, Olympic Gold medallist.

141. Passion of Success

Create a climate, where success becomes a burning passion.

142. Celebrate Success

When you win, the stars sing and you can dance all night.

143. Winners

The world loves winners. Moreover, winning is great fun!

144. Leaders Make

Leaders make a company or a country.

145. Transparency Pays

Development requires sound governance. Transparency pays.

146. Success in a New Country

Any business can succeed in any new country, if it adheres to the following simple guidelines:

    a) Make quality products,
    b) Create jobs,
    c) Value people,
    d) Pay all taxes,
    e) Know the Government,
    f) Avoid politics,
    g) Invest in the country,
    h) Be socially responsible.

147. Africa Liberalises

African countries have been through their sagas and are now opening doors to liberalisation, welcoming investments and making desperate attempts to occupy their rightful position in the community of nations. Many of them are opening their doors to investment.

148. Hard Work, Africa

Africa needs a lot more employment generation and economic prosperity. However, in this process, there will be pain, effort and some trauma. There are issues to be resolved, which are under review by governments. They are paying a price in terms of investing today, to get the results after some decades.

149. Scarcity to Plenty

Many African countries are evolving from agrarian to industrial economies. Some of them are moving from a time when they could not get a cake of soap freely, to becoming markets of abundance and competition.

150. A Strong Finance Minister

The Finance Minister had a direct style of putting his point across. When some persons raised objections to the purchase of a jet for the President of the country, he reacted publicly, "The President of the country cannot be expected to travel on a donkey!"

On another occasion, when some foreign donors tried to dictate the utilisation of their funds, he announced in Parliament, "They can keep their money, if we have to survive by eating grass, we will do so!"

151. When a Good Leader Goes

We stood for hours in the queue, in the night to salute him. I was moved by the nation's devotion for him. Millions of people waited patiently and endlessly, to pay their respects to him, in a disciplined manner. No police or army was required to manage the crowds. The former President of Tanzania, Mwalimu Julius Nyerere's spirit bound all the bleeding hearts. The river of mourners would just not end.

152. Searching for Growth Models

Many countries like China, Cuba, India and Tanzania were like Columbus, in the early years of development, trying to seek rapid growth but also experimenting with development models. Each found their own answers, gradually.

153. Dramatic Shift from Socialism

A dramatic shift from a socialistic pattern to a free market economy can be traumatic, in terms of employment and market dynamics.

154. Competition and Competitors

Competitors should battle in the streets, but remain personal and social friends! They should rejoice in each other's success.

155. Sub-distributors for Slums

Slums are ubiquitous in African towns. About 25 to 50 per cent of the population in many African towns lives in slums. Appoint sub-distributors in these areas to improve product reach.

156. Wholesaler Management

When any company architectures its own distribution system, the wholesalers have to be managed with sensitivity.

157. Market Battles, Warriors

Tough market battles are fought in every wholesale outlet, every shop, every village, every slum, on every wall through wall paintings. You have to transform the field force and staff into ferocious warriors. There can be no relenting.

The celebrated American General George Patton on inheriting a demoralised unit, commented, "They don't look like soldiers. They don't act like soldiers. Why should they fight like soldiers? The discipline's pretty poor. In about 15 minutes we're going to start turning these boys into fanatics, razors. They'll lose their fear."

158. Serve Customers

Customer-Service is the foundation of Brand Loyalty. The core of Customer-Service is the belief that the fundamental reason for the existence of an organisation is the satisfaction of customer needs. Then, the profits will pour in.

159. Everyone Is a Salesman

In a successful company, everyone in the team is a salesperson, irrespective of level or functional specialisation. If a company does not sell, there is no money to pay the bills! Smart companies tell their customers, we are open round the clock to service every order, however small the order may be. Look at Amazon. It works 365-366 days of the years, throughout the days and nights, across the globe.

160. Shake Hands with Consumers

We are paid to bring in revenues. Customers give us the revenues. So meet and talk to as many of them as possible – in the markets, in their offices, in the villages, anywhere, and make friends with them. Shake hands with the consumers in the country. Their needs and aspirations are the reasons for our existence. We get our salaries, as long as they keep buying our products.

161. Manage a Shop

When we launch mass-markets brands anywhere in the world, we have to reorient the minds of our team by exposing them to how consumers at the lower end of the market live. Therefore, we sent groups of our team to visit villages or slums or to run a rural shop. It means becoming a grass-root level entrepreneur.

162. Dance and Music, Africa

Africa loves music, dance and colours. Therefore, promotions with dance and music will mesmerise the crowds.

163. Local Production

Locally produced products get tremendous emotional support. There is pride amongst the locals for a product, being produced in their own country. The government is also delighted when hitherto silent factories start humming.

164. Contract Manufacturing

Whilst undertaking third-party production, it is imperative to ensure that we retain the quality control function. Production through existing units saves time and money.

165. Abhor Bureaucracy

Avoid stifling procedures and bottlenecks. Keep processes simple.

166. Plant Trees

Plant trees, fruits and vegetables in the compounds of the office, factories and warehouses. The plants grow and add to the enthusiasm of the staff.

167. For Africa

You have the best cashew, tobacco, gold.
Why not process them too?
Create more jobs!
Earn more foreign exchange for the treasury!
So, seize the opportunities,
And fulfil your destiny.

168. Sail On, Sail On

Folklore has it, that whenever Columbus was thwarted by the bureaucracy, the Spanish queen or the turbulent sea waters, he always exhorted "Sail on, Sail on, Sail on!"

169. The Price to Pay

"Provided he knew he had paid his uttermost farthing, how did it matter, how others judged the result."

- Dag Hammarskjöld, the former Secretary-General of the United Nations

170. Key: People

In building the Enterprise Culture, the key element is People.

171. Six Business Pillars

1) Build a distribution system to cover markets,
2) Tap the mass-markets,
3) Source local production,
4) Manage the environment,
5) Build teams and enterprise culture,
6) One last point: Strategy - "Complete Victory".

172. Challenge in Any Business

The challenge in any business often is, to take a group of ordinary people, forge them together by a common mission and deliver extraordinary results.

173. Leadership: Team Building

The job of the leader is to assimilate different cultures and nationalities into a sturdy team. People have to be woven and integrated into a strong team, dedicated to the company.

174. Think Differently

Inculcate one key lesson among all the team members: Break all the rules and think afresh. Think differently. No idea, however bizarre, is crazy.

175. Style of Operation

The style of operation in the future has to be open and democratic, with focus on teamwork. Traditional hierarchical structures will not deliver. We have to work as friends, though we have to be driven by the bottom line.

176. Tutor System

Introduce a tutor system for new, young managers. The tutors will play the role of management mentors.

177. Ten Golden Business Guidelines

1) Integrity: Write in stone,
2) Basics: Break, but not bend,
3) Evolve a vision – A dream!
4) Network thy "Government"
5) Forge people into a team,
6) Build with well-wishers,
7) Know thy consumers and markets,
8) Change paradigms,
9) Be Penny wise, Pounds follow,
10) Deliver success.

178. A Moral Compass

Saint Mother Teresa's Mission was our temple, mosque and church in Tanzania and Cote d'Ivoire. Hundreds of inmates, i.e. abandoned children of various ages, sick and unwanted old persons, live there, with human dignity, respect, clean beds, and wholesome food.

Whenever we needed people to commence new ventures like the bicycle brigade sales operations, I always approached the Sisters, as to whom we could gainfully employ. Like Blendila, who yet works with us, a part of the family. She is normally the first person to arrive in the office daily. She always smiles.

When we were deeply troubled, we retreated to the simple and tiny Chapel in Mother Teresa's Mission. It was a lagoon where we could find solace and solutions.

* * *

Many CEOs do not appreciate, that their primary job is to listen to their customers. They spend time monitoring the stock markets and share prices. They should realise that if they look after their customers, the stock market and share prices will look after the company.

Mr. Prakash Tandon, the first Indian Chairman of Hindustan Lever, would take his clean, white, neatly pressed handkerchief from his pocket and clean the Dalda vanaspati (hydrogenated fat) tins himself in the shops, to set an example to the selling team. He had no qualms about squatting on dusty gunny bags of sugar or wheat in the shops, to chat with shopkeepers, despite his fresh suit.

* * *

3

Selling To Billions Of Consumers

179. Sales: An Ignition Key

Sale is like the ignition key of a car. The car moves only when the key is deployed. Similarly, a company runs, as long as people buy its products.

180. First Customers

Distributors are the first customers of any company. Respect them. Razzle-dazzle them. Win them. To reach a billion or even a million consumers, a company needs strong distributors.

181. Steel Framework

A strong distributor network is a powerful steel framework for any company. Distributors are long-term partners of the company.

182. Sound Advice

"Our distributors are under severe pressures from local authorities, the trade and from consumers. You should heed these concerns. You should travel to these markets, talk to the distributors, understand their problems and help them to resolve the inconveniences. Treat them like your partners, take them into confidence," Mr. J.C. Chopra, the Marketing Director advised me, when I was trainee in the company.

183. Integrity with Distributors

To gain the respect of the distribution system, it is critical to maintain high levels of professional integrity in the entire system at all levels. One of the first lessons imparted to us was not to have any personal financial dealings with the distributors.

184. Reaching Consumers

India's voluminous market is scattered across about 4,000 urban cities and towns, and 640,850 villages. Therefore, to reach the 1.32 billion Indian consumers, through eight to ten million shopkeepers and grocers, is a daunting challenge. Similar challenges face companies in vast countries like China and Brazil.

185. Massive Variances

Selling to large countries like China, Brazil and India, is also complicated by the massive variances in cultures, consumption habits, income differentials, etc., within the countries. About 24 per cent of Indians, i.e. 276 million people subsist below the global poverty line, but the really wealthy Indians in cities could have very comfortable life-styles, spending USD 50,000 per month or more.

186. Pay for the Tea

My boss, Mr. R. Gopalakrishnan (then Sales and Marketing Manager – Foods, later Director, Tata Sons), told me that when the company was run by British managers, they were so fastidious about integrity, that they would even pay for the tea that they had at the office of the distributor.

187. Henry Ford's Advice

"It's not the employer who pays the salaries; it's the client," sums up Henry Ford very eloquently. Focus on Customer-Service.

188. Arab Wisdom

"If you want wisdom, visit many tents," is ancient Arab folklore. In every tent in the deserts, are mature and experienced men who have many lessons to impart. Thus, say the Arabs, the more tents you visit, the more will you learn. Similarly, the more shops you visit in the "bazaars" of any country, the more you will learn.

189. Sam Walton's Advice

"Our best ideas come from the shop-floors," commented Mr. Sam Walton, founder of the Walmart chain of stores, which has a revenue of USD 480 billion (2017), and 15,000 stores in 28 countries.

190. CEOs and Customers

Many CEOs do not appreciate, that their primary job is to listen to their customers. They spend time monitoring the stock markets and share prices. They should realise that if they look after their customers, the stock market and share prices will look after the company.

191. Clean Tins with White Handkerchief

Mr. Prakash Tandon, the first Indian Chairman of Hindustan Lever, would take his clean, white, neatly pressed handkerchief from his pocket and clean the Dalda vanaspati (hydrogenated fat) tins himself in the shops, to set an example to the selling team. He also had no qualms about squatting on dusty gunny bags of sugar or wheat in the shops, to chat with shopkeepers, despite his fresh suit.

192. White-Lux Story, Sensitivity

A shopkeeper in Indore suggested to Mr. Susim Datta, Chairman of Hindustan Lever, that we should launch a white Lux. Within a few weeks, the soap was launched! Mr. Susim Datta also asked me to visit the shopkeeper in Indore and present him with three tablets of white Lux with his compliments.

This type of sensitivity to feedback from shopkeepers and customers ensures winning brands. It also cements respect for the company.

193. Listen, Listen

A company, which listens to its shopkeepers, employees and consumers, is always successful.

194. Smart Companies

Smart companies know that they have to serve both segments, i.e. small shops and hypermarkets.

195. Slum Markets

About 20 to 30 per cent of the population of many urban townships in large towns like Mumbai, Delhi, Kolkata, Chennai, Sao Paulo, Rio de Janeiro, Lagos, Nairobi, etc., live in slums ("jhuggis" or "jhopdis"). They too, are customers.

196. Brand-Building: Multifunctional

Brand building is a multi-functional task. Brands are built every time a salesperson merchandises a tube of toothpaste or conducts a live washing demonstration for laundry soap or a frying demonstration for cooking oil, in a village square.

197. Street Lessons in Marketing

The Distributors and shopkeepers of Hindustan Lever Ltd., have taught me many valuable sales and marketing lessons. They have taught me as much as an MBA degree in marketing did.

198. Love the Wholesalers

The wholesaler is the fulcrum of the distribution system, as in most developing countries in Latin America, Africa, Middle East and Southeast Asia. Many companies service the entire market, through wholesalers. No company can thus afford to ignore or annoy the wholesalers.

199. Rural Markets

A consumer product company that does not operate in the rural markets in developing countries like India, Egypt, Pakistan, Kenya, Brazil, etc., will not grow.

200. Patience in Villages

Tapping the rural markets is tedious, exacting and expensive. It requires top management commitment, a mind-set through the company's management and field force and a clear budget. An immersion in the rural markets also requires patience, for sometimes results are slow in coming.

201. Marketing Etiquette

"Stop smoking! Never, never, ever smoke when you are making a sales call. If you need to smoke, take a short break and then resume your sales call," counselled my boss, Mr. D.B. Patel, the General Sales Manager of Foods.

202. Grocer, Company's Customer

The grocer is also a customer of any company. Only if he buys the products, stocks, merchandises and displays them, will the eventual consumer buy them. We have to be extraordinarily sensitive to the needs of the simple grocer, in every village or town.

203. Illiteracy and Intelligence

It is a mistake to take the simple, illiterate village grocer for granted and try to oversell to him or dump stocks in his shop. He knows what his consumers buy and how much they buy. We have to defer to his judgment. The grocer is intelligent, he is the person who sells and delivers our products to the consumers at all times.

204. Wednesday? Bazaar!

It has been my practice, whenever I have managed a business, to spend every Wednesday in the market, meeting customers and having face-to-face discussions with them about products, market trends, competition activity, etc. The visits keep me updated about the market, and also keep my teams sharp.

205. Shopping Revolution

The entry of large operators like Carrefour, IKEA, Tesco, etc., has revolutionised shopping experiences and patterns in many countries and continents in the world like China, Latin America, Middle East, etc.

206. Welcome Hypermarkets

In many developing countries, Foreign Direct Investment (FDI) in retail will enable massive investments in supply chain structures, reduce and stabilise prices, ensure improved training and development of staff and hygienic work environments. The opposition to Foreign Direct Investment in the retail business by political parties in some countries, could be regressive.

207. Hypermarkets, Consumer Benefits

Hypermarkets will provide consumers with better and fresher choices, in all product categories.

208. Hygiene, Hygiene

Municipal authorities abroad, regularly visit shops in many countries to ensure adherence to hygiene standards. I was getting a haircut in Dubai. Municipal officers visited the saloon, to tutor the hairdresser on the importance of keeping the premises tidy and using gloves. Such quality enforcement should be initiated in developing countries, across retail outlets, especially in outlets selling food products.

209. Miles to Go

The modern trade in India and many developing countries, is miniscule in size and impact. It has many miles to go, before it can become a significant contributor to the economy or the shoppers' pleasure.

210. Revere Your People

"Take away my factories, my plants, take away my railroads, my ships, my transportation; take away my money, strip me of all these, but leave me my men and in two or three years, I will have them all again," asserted Andrew Carnegie, the Scottish-American industrialist, who led the enormous expansion of the American steel industry in the late 19th century.

211. Value Sales Staff

Many companies take their field force, i.e. sales representatives for granted. When a company loses its field force, it loses years of training and experience. More important, it loses the relationships, which the field force has with shopkeepers.

212. Honour, Honour

Honour your top achievers with money, glory, medals, certificates and awards. Then, see your sales graphs climb north.

213. Share Options

Take share options down to the field force and see the sales gallop.

214. Pillars of a Business

The salespersons of any business are its pillars. Tinker around with the pillars and the building starts wobbling.

215. Lonely Life

Selling is a lonely process. It is important for the company to provide salespersons with strong support, through frequent contacts and communications.

216. Demoralisation and Locust

A demoralised field force in a company, is like locust eating away the framework of a building, slowly and silently. So, care for your salespersons.

217. Cluttered Shops

Shops in countries like India and other developing countries like Egypt, Peru, Vietnam, etc., are amongst the most cluttered in the world.

218. Rivet Attention, in Crowd

Smart companies try to ensure that their brands are well shelved and merchandised in the shop, however crowded it may be. The goal is simple: to rivet the attention of the shopper and sell the product.

219. Paint the Slums

We literally took a colossal tin of green paint and poured it all over Dharavi (a slum) turning it green, with massive displays of the green colour packs, supported by wall and shop paintings when we launched a green-coloured brand, Wheel. It worked wonders.

220. Staff for Slum Operations

It is provident to recruit sales staff from the slums, to service these markets. They know the buying habits of consumers, the routes and the traders. Their local knowledge is immensely useful.

221. Costs and Value

Companies constantly evaluate how much the field force and distribution apparatus costs and what value they add.

222. Productivity

Ensuring high productivities in callage, success rates and lines per call, maximises field force contributions.

223. Internet in Villages

Internet in the villages, across developing countries, will generate a huge opportunity for brands and marketers in the villages, where establishing a physical presence is still an infrastructural challenge.

224. World Travels to Villages

"I have an "Esmart" (smart) phone. I spend an hour daily on the Internet, on how to improve my wheat crop in the fields," Rajesh says. The mobile phone has revolutionised his life in a tiny village in India's largest state. "The world has travelled to me, via my phone," he proclaims.

225. Telecom's Rural Revolution

The telecom revolution in the villages of Asia and Africa could yield significant advantages in enhancing productivity and improving the quality of life in the villages. Farmers can access information on how to augment crop productivity. They will be better informed on prices of the rice or maize that they grow.

226. Rural Heartbeats

Mahatma Gandhi had opined, "India's heart beats in its villages. Now 4G, and very soon, 5G smart technologies phones, will make the heartbeats of villagers resound across countries and continents.

227. Best Cup of Tea in World

The shopkeeper does not need the company. The company needs him. So if he offers an over-sugared cup of tea, sip it as if it was the best cup of tea in the world.

* * *

Amazon is one of the most successful companies in the world, for its highly focussed customer orientation and service. Amazon has developed Customer-Service into a fine art through customer anticipation and a science through information technology. You do not meet an Amazon salesperson, yet they provide superior service.

A prerequisite to Customer-Servicing, is that the company has to be employee friendly. No company should ever forget that its employees are its customers too. Disgruntled employees are not going to make that "little" extra effort, which makes the vital "difference" in serving a customer.

* * *

4

Customer-Service Across Markets

228. Focus on Customer-Service

Woo the customer. Delight him. Tantalise her.

229. Products Must Deliver

Customer-Service is the timely anticipation and comprehensive satisfaction of the needs of the consumer. A product is not a mere object. It is a promise to fulfil a need, to meet a hope. Any product, which fails to fulfil its promised performance, is tantamount to being deceitful to the customer.

230. Customer-Service and Profits

The organisation should believe that satisfying its customers is its key objective, its raison d'être. The core of Customer-Service orientation is the belief that the fundamental reason for the existence of an organisation is the satisfaction of customer needs. In the process of fulfilling its customers' needs, the organisation will also make a profit.

231. Profits: Logical Outcome

Profits are a logical outcome of customer satisfaction.

232. Profits and Quality

Profits are not independent of product quality and customer satisfaction.

233. Marks and Spencer

Companies, which have made Customer-Service the fulcrum of their business activities, have flourished in all parts of the world. Consider the case of Marks and Spencer. Their chain of stores enjoys an enviable reputation across the world.

234. Operating Philosophy

As an operating philosophy, Customer-Service should go all the way back to the sales organisation, marketing department and the production floor itself.

235. Permeate All-Around

Customer-Service is a philosophy, which has to permeate every single stage, phase and process, in every functional department of the company.

236. Amazon's Success

Amazon is one of the most successful companies in the world, for its highly focussed customer orientation and service. Amazon has developed Customer-Service into a fine art through customer anticipation and a science through information technology. You do not meet an Amazon salesperson, yet they provide superior service.

237. Information Technology and Service

The adroit and smart use of information technology is revolutionising Customer-Service across the world.

238. Global Discontinuities

a) End of the cold war and disintegration of the USSR.
b) Globalisation of the economies of the world.
c) Advances in telecommunications, satellite, Internet, mobile phones, etc., have shrunk the world. The world has become smaller.
d) Higher degrees of information dissemination, awareness among consumers across the world.
e) Liberalisation of regulations in East Europe, China and third world countries.
f) Renewed interest among corporations in the West in investing in the third world countries, considering the vast untapped potential markets like India, China, Vietnam, etc.

239. Free Market System

Perhaps the most significant development of the last few decades, has been the end of the cold war and the uncrowned victory of the free market system of managing an economy. Foreign investment and technology is likely to flow more freely across national frontiers, in the future.

240. Exceed Expectations

Smart companies will exceed the service expectations of their customers.

241. Distributors as Customers

The distributor of the company should be seen as the first customer. Distributors too, are customers. They too, have to be serviced.

242. Calibrate Norms

Restructuring operations in a company to underscore Customer-Service also implies setting quantitative norms and standards, which calibrate Customer-Servicing. Managers in all the departments should be evaluated on their attitude and ability to service the customer.

243. Employees as Customers

A prerequisite to Customer-Servicing, is that the company has to be employee friendly. No company should ever forget that its employees are its customers too. Disgruntled employees are not going to make that "little" extra effort, which makes the vital "difference" in serving a customer.

244. Employee Friendly

If a company intends being Customer-Service oriented, it has to be first, employee-friendly.

245. Liberalisation and Service

Liberalisation created competition. To win in a competitive scenario, companies have to woo and seduce the customer.

246. Next Few Decades

The next few decades will be characterised by:

a) Greater awareness of brands and options due to increased penetration of media like TV, press, radio, Internet, etc.
b) Augmented demand for electronic products (TVs, Mobiles, etc.) and for basic consumer products like groceries, toiletries, convenience products (primus stoves, electric irons, etc.) in the urban and rural markets.
c) Urban and rural consumers will spend more on consumer products, which offer convenience, time savings, status, etc.
d) Global consumers will have higher expectations in terms of quality and performance.
e) Availability of products made abroad or produced locally, under foreign franchise arrangements will increase.
f) Consumer forums will be proactive in redressing the grievances of consumers.

247. Stop the Production Line!

Sony was one of the few companies in the world, where the factory floor worker had the right to stop the production line, if he considered the quality of the product unsatisfactory. Now, this is Customer-Service. The customer is so supreme, that an ordinary worker is empowered to stop the production line, if in his judgment, the product is not good enough for the ultimate consumer.

248. Standard Consumer Aspirations

Global satellite TV programmes are contributing to the standardisation of consumer aspirations and products across national frontiers.

249. Survival Depends on Service

More choices, mean more competition. Only the fittest will survive. The fittest will be those, who can maximise customer satisfaction. Businesses, which are incapable of Customer-Service, will not survive.

250. Japanese Edge

The secret behind the success of many Japanese electronics companies like Sony, Canon, etc. has been their ceaseless and uncanny ability to constantly comprehend and meet customer needs.

251. Product Availability

If a company has generated demand for a product through advertising and publicity, customers expect the product to be widely available at retail outlets.

252. Robust Packaging

A customer expects the company to deliver the product in packaging that is robust and protects the contents. It should also be pilfer proof.

253. Product Information

Increasingly, customers will demand more information about the product. They may even seek information about the manufacturing technology.

254. Lip-service Only

Many organisations render mere lip-service to Customer-Service. Customer-Service will improve with augmented competition.

255. Companies Too, Die

"Propping up ailing giants, as governments everywhere are constantly asked to do, only delays the final deathbed scene, as well as the birth of the new. Companies are not enduring institutions. Nor should they be." (The Economist).

256. The Human Touch

In Ghana and Uganda, if a company forgets to give a small Christmas present to its distributors, it is taken as a major affront and a lapse in customer-relationship and service. Even a greeting card from the company at festival times, can make a distributor happy. The human touch matters.

* * *

Great leaders are achievers. They are aware of their capabilities. They can extend their personalities and audience impressions through planning, visualising, acting, painstaking effort and sheer sacrifice.

Most Hollywood actors, however senior they are, participate in auditions, before getting plum roles. Even actors of the stature of Marlon Brando had to audition for his role in the epic movie, "Godfather".

* * *.

5

Anatomy Of Leadership

Understanding Leadership

257. Walking With

Learn to walk with the Royalty and the forlorn with equal ease.

258. Leaders Transform People

Leadership provides organisations with vision. It also propels the organisation towards change. Leaders should be able to transform their followers into leaders in their own departments or constituencies. Then they should transform these local leaders into agents of change, to execute the enterprise vision into reality.

259. Leaders Have to be Painters

Leaders know that it is important to have a vision and communicate it to their teams. A leader thus has to be an artist, a painter. He has draw the picture of the future and sell it to his team to get their commitment.

260. What Leaders Do

The foremost task of leaders is to develop a vision for the enterprise for the future. They should communicate and institutionalise the vision among the team members. Leaders have to ceaselessly scan the environment, to constantly review changes in the political, economic and technological scenarios. Then they review how to keep repositioning the enterprise to meet its goals.

261. Leaders Have To Be Detailed, Too

Great leaders also know that vision is not enough. Execution is critical. In execution every element of the plan is important. We have heard the proverb "For want of a nail, the Kingdom was lost." This comes from a longer proverb about a battle during which the loss of a nail in a horseshoe leads to the loss of a horse, which leads to the loss of the rider, which leads to the loss of the battle, which in turn leads to the loss of a whole kingdom.

The great American General George Patton who won many battles in World War II, was obsessed with details. He exhorted his officers to ensure that all the soldiers had warm socks to protect their feet, when they went into battle.

262. Complex Times

The major challenge characterising modern times is complexity. Social media has changed the way people behave across the world. Artificial Intelligence is likely to usher unforeseen changes. Today's leaders have to grapple with new intricacies every day.

263. Unprecedented Scrutiny

The social media and information explosion has led to leaders being subjected to unprecedented scrutiny. There is tremendous premium attached to credibility. Leaders are under constant analysis and any lapse in their official or personal demeanour, is picked up and magnified.

264. Bye-Bye Privacy

A leadership has to sacrifice his privacy, in a time when social media, consumer groups, environment awareness, governments' regulations, all permit a citizen to question and challenge authority. How much privacy does President Donald Trump or any other President or Prime Minister in the world have? Leaders are becoming public property now.

265. Leadership Is Integrity

Mr. T. Thomas, the Chairman of Hindustan Lever Ltd., the largest FMCG business, selling some billions of tablets of soap every year, was concerned whether we had paid a distributor for the five tablets, we had taken from him, for an official visit in the rural areas. Such professionalism in dealing with the trade builds robust reputations.

266. Manage Yourself First

Those who wish to lead must first manage themselves. A sloppy leader will lose credibility. A good leader is always in command of himself. Leaders have to combine efficiency with a high degree of effectiveness. Their vision should be so ethereal and powerful, that they should be able to guide and inspire their followers. Mahatma Gandhi's loft vision of a free India, inspired millions in the cities and villages.

267. Concentration

Leaders are able to concentrate on important tasks. They allocate adequate times to major goals and go for them. They set challenging goals and inspire their teams to pursue them with dedication, imagination and creativity. The pursuit of an agenda brings out the best in the leaders and their teams.

268. Compelling Communicators

Effective leaders are enthralling communicators. They can describe their visions to their teams, to inspire enthusiasm and commitment in them. Leaders may be articulate, or they may be men of few words; either way, they are effective.

269. Leaders Should Be Predictable

A leader should make his values, position, goals known to his team. Then he should stay the course. Predictable and persistent leaders inspire followers. Their total dedication inspires trust in their teams. When everything is against them, they fight one more round. They never give up.

270. Leaders Read, Learn

Rubert Murdoch, Warren Buffett, Bill Gates, Jeffrey Bezos, Mark Zuckerberg are all great readers. They pay sharp attention to new technologies and emerging realities. Great leaders are constant learners.

271. Vision to Actions

Leaders are as powerful as the ideas they communicate. They also have to act, to deliver the vision, through actions. Visions cannot be enforced or dictated by power or coercion in an enterprise or a team. The leader has to persuade his followers to dedicated action. "No words, but action," is the hymn of any great leader.

272. Leader As Architect

The effective leader has to amass the vision of the future. This is his basic and prime responsibility. It cannot be diluted or delegated. The leader develops visions based on his experiences, his philosophy, style and his instincts. Then, he has to marshal the organisation to accept his revelation and act on it.

273. Ordinary Men

Most leaders are born ordinary. Yet many rise to positions whereby they determine the destinies of communities and corporations. Such leaders believe in persistence, self-introspection, life-long education and willingness to take risks. They know that they may suffer setbacks. Despite losses, they remain committed and steady. They welcome adversities and challenges. They are charismatic. They are also brilliant time-managers.

274. Leaders Search for Strengths

Leaders are constantly searching for strengths when there may be none. Leaders learn to draw water out of stones. They always see a solution.

275. Grandstanding and Fruit-Salad

Leadership is not just grandstanding. Good leaders know that every goal has to be splintered into smaller tasks and each piece tackled. The renowned Guru of Method Acting, Mr. Lee Strasberg advises that acquisition of acting or leadership skills, is similar to preparing a dish of fruit salad. Each fruit has to be washed, peeled, cut one at a time. He further expounds that you cannot get a plate of fruit salad by just ordering the fruits or wishing for it. Each fruit will have to be selected, peeled and cut. And, then mixed in a certain proportion to get the right taste and colour. He compares the acquisition of acting or leadership skills, to the making of fruit salad. Mr. Strasberg would know, having trained actors and stars like Kim Hunter, Marilyn Monroe, Marlon Brando, Dustin Hoffman and Al Pacino.

Becoming a Leader

276. Leaders Evolve

Leaders are made, not born. No leader sets out to be a leader. He merely endeavours to express himself freely to achieve a mission. Mahatma Gandhi did not set out to be a leader. He merely wanted an equitable deal for the Indians in South Africa. Later he wanted the Indians in India to be free and live their own lives. Mahatma Gandhi continued to evolve throughout his life, with the inspiring dream of a free India. Later, Reverend Martin Luther King Jr. followed his philosophy of non-violence in the USA.

277. Discipline Is Valuable in Life

All great achievements are due to strong disciplines. Great battles are also won due to discipline. The celebrated American General George Patton was a great believer and enforcer of discipline, as can be seen from the following dialogue, from the classic movie "Patton", between General Patton and a cook at the barracks:

> "Cook: Up bright and early, general? Breakfast?
>
> Patton: Have all my officers finished breakfast?
>
> Cook: We're open from 6 till 8. Most of the officers are just coming in, sir.
>
> Patton: Please inform these officers the mess hall is closed.
>
> Cook: But, sir! It's only a quarter to 8.
>
> Patton: From now on, you will open at 6 and no one will be admitted after 6:15. Where are your leggings?
>
> Cook: Leggings? Well, hell, general, sir, I'm a cook.
>
> Patton: You're a soldier. $20 fine. Gentlemen, from this moment any man, without leggings, without a helmet, without a tie, any man with unshined shoes or soiled uniform, is going to be skinned. This is a barracks. It's not a bordello.

278. Battle, Yourself

There is no battle, until the salespersons and soldiers are willing to fight for you, or, you go into battle yourself.

279. Ability To Transform

Leaders are ceaselessly reviewing the strengths and weaknesses of their teams and drawing plans to brace skills. They build on capabilities. They believe that any human being can transform himself, through application. Leaders are like Professor Henry Higgins (Rex Harrison) in "My Fair Lady" who can transform a coarse and craggy Cockney flower-girl Eliza Doolittle (Audrey Hepburn) into a Royal Princess.

280. Generating Trust

People follow a leader because there is an honest belief in the person. President Richard Nixon of the USA had to resign, because the people did not trust him after the Watergate scandal. Prime Minister Tony Blair of UK also had to ease himself out, after people thought that he led them into an avoidable war in Iraq, without concrete evidence of the presence of weapons of mass destruction.

281. Action Orientation

A key element in becoming an effective leader is action-orientation. Reflection by itself is not enough. Thinking does not deliver results. Action does. So a leader must be action driven.

282. Deliver Results

Strategy discussions are fantastic. Eventually a company wants money delivered. So ultimately a leader has to roll up his sleeves and deliver results on the ground.

283. Competence and Questions

Leadership is not an esoteric, exalted, rarefied skill. It demands strong professional competence in all areas like marketing, production, personnel and finance. The leader must develop robust functional skills in all areas of work. The CEO may not know all the answers, but he should know the right questions to ask.

284. Delivery, Key Quality for Leader

A key leadership quality is the ability to deliver results. No leader can continue unless he delivers quantifiable results. Chairmen of companies, Prime Ministers and Presidents of corporations have had to pack their trunks and go, because they could not deliver on their promises to their constituents.

285. Organisations Build Leaders

Organisations with their guidelines, rules, and precedents can side-line entrepreneurship and initiative. Some techniques employed by companies to develop potential leaders are establishing venture capital pools or focussed businesses, to enable them to start and manage tough enterprises.

At Hindustan Lever Ltd., where I worked for some decades, managers (including myself) were often sent to work in the Animal Feeds Business. The division manufactured feeds for poultry and animals like cows, buffaloes, rabbits, horses and even monkeys. It was a low margin business, managed in a very cost-effective manner, located in the interior towns. The biggest problem was that the eventual consumer, the horse or the buffalo was not able to talk to me and tell me what it wanted. How do you make food for customers, who cannot talk to you and tell you what they want? "If a manager can work in the Animal Feeds Business, he can work anywhere," opined a former Chairman of the Company.

286. A Polite Chairman

We were having cocktails one evening. After making all the arrangements, I slid out quietly to check on the dinner settings. I returned after 20 minutes and the Chairman Mr. T. Thomas, asked me, "We are waiting for you. Where were you?" He had asked everyone to hold on to their drinks, until I joined the group. I was a rookie trainee and did not even expect to be noticed. I became his fan.

287. A Wise Leader

The Chairman had a razor-sharp mind and could cut through jargon, to identify the key issue. He deciphered people very easily and thoroughly. He could read the eyes and mind of a person and the answers to his questions, even before the other person could respond to a query. It was uncanny and chilling.

288. Writing with a Pencil

The Chairman's annual speeches were classics. They were in great demand in the Government. He hand-wrote his speeches with a pencil. Then his personal assistant, Mrs. Amy Kharas typed them out for him.

289. The Small Notebook

Mr. Thomas, the Chairman always kept a small notebook in his upper shirt pocket. Whenever he travelled, he would jot down important points, which needed action or follow-up, on his return to his office. We were delighted when he jotted any of our requests or suggestions in his small notebook. We knew, once a point had a place in his small notebook, action was imminent.

290. Be Cool

On a visit from London, a Chairman took me aside and said, "You resigned and stayed back. People may be cold to you. Do not let that bother you." A leader always makes time for his people and knows how to comfort or reassure them.

291. Winter Time

It was winter. Dusk was descending as early as 6 pm. He turned towards me and said almost philosophically, "In this city we have fought many battles. I am glad that the Government yet calls me for advice. However, I know that by the time I return from my London posting, people here may forget me. They will not seek my advice." I told him, this was not true. "With your wealth of experience, your counsel will always be valued," I responded. He kept looking out of the car window wistfully, as the dusk became denser.

292. Foresight, See Ahead

A good leader sees ahead. He plans and thinks much before the actual trouble arises. He outlines his course of action under various circumstances in advance, so that no struggle catches him unawares.

293. Repositioning Yourself

Great leaders are achievers. They are aware of their capabilities. They can extend their personalities through planning, visualising, acting, painstaking effort and sheer sacrifice. Many of them have been through a phase of career "dip" and undertake "repositioning" or "remanufacturing" involving training, coaching and polishing. Most Hollywood actors, however senior they are, attend refresher programmes and participate in auditions, before getting plum roles. Even actors of the stature of Marlon Brando had to audition for his role in the epic movie, "Godfather". So even great actors keep retraining themselves.

294. Manufacturing Success

"Visibility" and "celebrity-status" can be manufactured in entertainment, sports, business, politics and religion through the rigorous application of marketing principles and techniques. The images of personalities are designed to meet the expectations of the audience (market). The aspirants are transfigured in studios, beauty parlours, coaching sessions (factories) and are taught everything from hygiene to managing interviews, even how to greet people at a railway station or an airport. Celebrity aspirants have to learn to manage their social media also, e.g. Facebook, Twitter, etc.

Most aspirants for the job of the President of the USA are perfectly polished in their personal presentation, attire, public comments, including their white shining teeth. They are coached to present themselves as global leaders.

295. Personality Positioning

In a competitive world, merely possessing the requisite professional skills, is not enough to guarantee success. How people project and position themselves, will distinguish the celebrities from the multitude of professionals. President Vladimir Putin takes every opportunity to position himself as a macho president to the Russian people. He rides horses bare-chested, goes fishing, sailing, etc., showing he has the energy to captain the country.

296. Business Celebrities

The plethora of business magazines across the world, has also added to the insatiable hunger for news about businessmen. Business leaders are being advised to seek the public limelight rather than shun it, to boost their own stock and that of their companies.

297. Fish-Tank Life

Leaders and celebrities have no privacy. Number One is a lonely position, anywhere. Leaders live in transparent fish-tanks. A wee sordid incident can mar their image permanently. Their private tensions are more stressful due to the lack of genuine friends. In many countries business leaders are constantly under fear of being kidnapped. Senior personnel of multinationals, have armed guards protecting them from being kidnapped in some countries in Latin America. However, for this enforced loneliness, leaders enjoy fame and even affluence.

298. Life, Not Just Slick

Fame and success do not kiss the feet of all those who are willing to play the orchestra, for these two vain mistresses. There has to be content, basic talent and solid performance. You cannot manipulate your success and high public visibility by learning how to walk and talk, by merely transforming the personality, determining the desired image and employing suitable media like television, press, agents, etc. Ultimately a leader has to deliver results and moneys.

299. Who Is a Leader?

Most of us aspire to be leaders in our groups, societies, states and nation. A leader is a person who makes others follow him by virtue of the strength of his views, personality and foresight. He gives the people a sense of direction at a time when they face difficulties and do not know which way to go. In every nation there is a tremendous need for leaders who can guide people towards political stability and economic well-being. In every field i.e. politics, business, commerce, industry, labour and universities, we need men of intelligence and competence who have the strength of character and will to give a new direction to the flow of events.

300. Selflessness

This is the essence of leadership, for every leader gives a part or all of his time, energy, activity, to guide and help others. This is essential because if the purpose of the leader is only to reap a harvest for himself, sooner or later, if the people are educated and conscious, they will replace him.

301. Involvement of a Leader

Unless a leader is involved with the issue himself, he will not be able to inspire others to action on that issue. He must be committed to the particular cause and be enthusiastic. Then only will he be able to arouse genuine concern among his followers. US President Abraham Lincoln was able to inspire his followers, during the American Civil War, because he believed in his cause, as expounded in the Gettysburg address, *"It is rather for us to be here dedicated to the great task remaining before us—that from these honoured dead (soldiers who sacrificed their lives) we take increased devotion to that cause for which they gave the last full measure of devotion—that we here highly resolve that these dead shall not have died in vain—that this nation, under God, shall have a new birth of freedom—and that government of the people, by the people, for the people, shall not perish from the earth."*

302. Courage and Character

If the leader has the character to distinguish right from wrong, he must have the courage to take a stand that may be disapproved by the people, but may be justified by his conscience. President Kennedy's book, "Profiles in Courage" gives vivid biographical sketches of leaders who did not sacrifice their convictions at the altar of popularity.

303. Leadership: Grit and Determination

Indians worship Mahendra Singh Dhoni, the former Captain of the Indian cricket team, for his leadership and maturity. When he was young he could not even afford to buy a bat. Now he is the king of hearts in the country.

It sends a powerful message that with talent and determination anyone is unstoppable.

304. Leadership Demands Intelligence

Leadership demands quick calculation, decision and adjustment in cases of emergency. Unless a person has the mental equipment to weigh and judge facts objectively and sift fact and fiction, his decisions will not be reliable. Nevertheless integrity and conviction are equally important. A humble leader, who has not seen the wide big world, can also inspire action with his convictions.

305. Responsibility With Authority

The general tendency among most people who aspire to be leaders is to demand the maximum authority and minimum responsibility. The leader who does not face the consequences of his decisions and actions will never enjoy the confidence of his fellowmen. Responsibility must be proportionate to authority. In fact, we must learn to welcome responsibilities, since they give us an opportunity to exercise our skills and become more self-confident.

306. Toughness in Mind and Body

The potential leader must be tough in mind and body. He must be a tough-minded optimist. Unless he can shed the blanket of confusion and despair, he will not be able to guide his fellowmen. Since leadership demands strenuous effort, a good leader will maintain a healthy physique or he will be at a disadvantage. Leadership is a tough job, requiring toughness of mind and body. President Barack Obama was very particular about his morning work-out to keep fit. He adhered to his schedule even when travelling aboard Air Force One.

307. Leadership: An Art

Leadership is definitely an art. It can be acquired. It is erroneous to say that all great leaders are born, or that all great leaders are the creatures of circumstances. If we feel strongly about any issue, it becomes our duty to make our fellowmen aware of the potential dangers or benefits accruing from a certain course of action. This demands leadership. Each person should endeavour to become a leader, in college, university, profession, community and society and expend his energies to the task of changing things for the better. The world's numerous problems demand leaders. And it is our responsibility to meet this demand.

It is the spirit of serving fellow men that inspired many men and made them leaders of mankind.

* * *

Respect the Retail Shop like a Temple.

A retailer can frequently make or break a new brand, depending on the recommendation he gives about it, to his regular and trusted consumers.

Shopkeepers and distributors can teach many valuable sales and marketing lessons, much more than an MBA degree in marketing can.

* * *

6

Power of A Retailer

308. Birbal's Advice

"Baniyon Se Seyano, So Diwano." (He, who claims that he is more astute than a grocer, is a fool.)

- Counsellor Birbal to Emperor Akbar (1556-1605)

309. Shop Is a Temple

Respect the Retail Shop like a Temple.

310. Tribute to Enterprise

A small retailer even in the remote villages in India, Kenya, Nigeria, Brazil, Colombia, Peru, Vietnam, Myanmar, etc., is able to meet the manifold basic requirements of his consumers be it soaps, toothpaste, biscuits, buckets, plastic pipes, fertilisers or cosmetics. The fact that such consumer products are available in the villages in most developing countries is a tribute to the enterprise and the dynamism of the retailing community and the intensive distribution systems that have evolved.

311. Practical MBA

Shopkeepers and distributors can teach many valuable sales and marketing lessons, much more than an MBA degree in marketing can.

312. Critical Link

Companies involved in the marketing of consumer products have realised that the retailer is the critical link in selling any product to the consumer. No marketing plan for any consumer product can be complete, if it ignores the incentives that have to be offered to the retailer to make him stock and promote the product. It is the special equation that a retailer enjoys with his customers, that makes him a focus for any marketing company.

313. Retailer Power

A retailer can frequently make or break a new brand, depending on the recommendation he gives about it, to his regular and trusted consumers.

314. Women as Retailers

The retail trade is changing constantly due to evolving technologies and cultures. A significant change is that in many countries like Southeast Asia, Latin America and Africa, women are managing shops and small supermarkets. It is quite common to see rows of shops being managed by women in Sao Paulo, Lima, Lagos, Nairobi, Manila, Hanoi, etc.

315. Low Cost Distribution

The direct linkage of the companies to the retail trade has resulted in low cost distribution systems, which ensures the widespread availability of consumer products even in the remotest villages.

316. Neighbourhood Markets

In Africa, retailers in Neighbourhood markets continue to be a major draw. These are clusters of small retailers, near residential localities. Neighbourhood markets principally sell on cash, since they sell directly to consumers. Their Unique Selling Proposition can be summed in one word "Fresh", since their focus is to sell fresh meat, fish, vegetables and fruits, for daily use.

317. Table-Top Retailers

Table-Top markets, are retail markets on tables. This is a particular phenomenon of African markets e.g. Kenya, Tanzania, Uganda, Nigeria, etc. Table-Top markets can also be observed in Caribbean markets like Haiti, Dominican Republic and other West Indies markets. A typical selling table could be four feet by six feet, or smaller, i.e. three feet by two feet. Table-Top markets principally sell fresh produce of meats, fish, fruits and vegetables.

318. Information Technology

Information technology has revolutionised the operations of small retailers also. Many of them are literally online with the distributors of companies and have automatic replenishment systems. Small grocers in towns are also becoming sophisticated in inventory management and are thus acquiring more power and knowledge.

319. Unique Retailer Equation

The equation, which the retailer enjoys with his consumers, is unique. In most Western countries, shopping is a very impersonal activity. The supermarket owner or manager does not meet his clientele and unlike the small retailer, he cannot directly contribute to the sales of a brand.

320. Massage the Retailer

Companies strive to convince retailers about the quality of their products. When a new toilet soap was launched, a company distributed a tablet free to every shopkeeper in town. The company hoped that the shopkeeper would use the soap and then recommend it confidently to his customers.

321. Smell the Lemon

When a new lemon-perfumed scouring powder was launched in Africa, the sales representatives carried a lemon in one hand and an open packet of the powder in the other hand. They made every shopkeeper in town smell the lemon and then the powder to convince them, about the abundance of lemon perfume in the cleaning powder.

322. Direct Links

To dilute the capacity of the wholesaler to manipulate the market for short term profiteering, companies have established direct linkages with the retailers. These companies appoint distributors and stockists, who book orders directly from retailers and supply stocks to them.

323. Turnover, A Secret

A secret which the retailer guards fiercely even from his spouse is his annual turnover. There are a large number of sundry items, which the retailer stocks and sells, of which he does not keep a strict inventory. He keeps their accounts in his mind only. The tax-inspector is unable to pinpoint the exact turnover or profit of a small shopkeeper or retailer, in developing countries.

324. Retailers' Credit Flexibility

Many retailers extend credit to their customers for periods ranging from 15 to 30 days. The practice of extending credit is prevalent across developing countries. It is also common in towns and markets where the bulk of the clientele comprises of the salaried class.

325. Role of Wholesalers

The wholesalers play a very vital role in distributing a large number of products in developing countries like India, Egypt, Brazil, Nigeria, Vietnam, etc. Their strength is that they possess large amounts of finance, which enable them to sell their products to the retail trade on credit, for periods extending from one to four weeks.

326. Wholesalers and Prices

The pivotal role of the wholesaler in the distribution network is fraught with dangers. Since the wholesaler has the finance and therefore, the "holding capacity", he is in a position to create artificial shortages by hoarding stocks. Two or three wholesalers can easily create an artificial scarcity.

327. Wholesalers Crucial

In many countries, in the Middle East, Latin America, Africa, etc., the wholesalers continue to be the prime channel for distributing consumer products. Multinational companies like Nestle, Unilever, Procter & Gamble, etc., have made efforts to build distributor system in these countries. However many local companies continue to operate through wholesalers.

328. Shopping: Social Activity

Shopping for consumer products and daily necessities will continue to be a social activity, not merely a functional chore. Quite frequently two or three homemakers visit the market in a group, even for shopping essential convenience items or fruits and vegetables.

329. Supermarkets, Working Women

Supermarkets always receive a substantial fillip when the majority of women are working and are pressed for time.

330. Traditional Retail to Continue

In the next many decades, the paramount position of the shopkeeper retailer will not be impacted by supermarkets or cooperative stores surfacing in India, Latin America, Southeast Asia or Africa.

331. Next Generation, Retailers

Most retailers complain that once their children are educated, they are reluctant to sit in the shop or carry on the family business of retailing. They are keen on taking up white-collar jobs. Time will tell how retailing traditions will adapt to meet this new social challenge.

* * *

The second person on this planet was the first person to enter the profession of salesmanship. For, Eve perceived certain needs in Adam and "sold" him the "idea" of eating the fruit of the Forbidden Tree. As Adam devoured the fruit, the first seeds of salesmanship were sown. The history of salesmanship, thus, commences with the birth of our planet and civilisation.

* * *

7

Universal Value Of A Salesman

Salesman and Selling

332. The Mouse-Trap

Mr. James Henry Atkinson, who invented the mouse-trap in 1897, said, "Build a better mouse-trap and the world will beat a path to your door." However, he did not realise that whilst advertising would help him to generate awareness about the mouse-trap, without a salesman his mouse-trap would adorn only his own doorstep.

333. Selling, Makes it Happen

The observation that "Nothing happens until somebody sells something" is true since generations. All the great discoverers of our world achieved success and recognition only when they were able to sell their inventions. Edison had to light an office building free of charge. Morse had to plead before ten Congresses to look at his telegraph. King Gillette took five years to sell his first seven safety razors.

334. Salesman: an Ignition

The salesman can justifiably be likened to Ford's ignition key, which sparks the relationship between the inventor of a product and the eventual customer.

335. Adam and Eve

The second person on this planet was the first person to enter the profession of salesmanship. For, Eve perceived certain needs in Adam and "sold" him the "idea" of eating the fruit of the Forbidden Tree. As Adam devoured the fruit, the first seeds of salesmanship were sown. The history of salesmanship, thus, commences with the birth of our planet and civilisation.

336. Historical Evolution

Salesmanship has lubricated the wheels of societies and economies since time immemorial. It is an ancient art.

337. Salespersons, Economic Institutions

The history of the evolution of salesmanship through centuries has thus been intertwined with advances in transportation, communication, production methods, banking facilities and is a significant phase of economic history. Over the years, the salesman has become an economic institution in society and selling has become a paramount function.

338. Selling, Persuasive Activity

Selling is also an utterly human and persuasive activity, performed by a human being, the salesman. The salesman is thus the most critical link in the flow of goods from factories to homes.

339. Selling: Human Persuasion

The salesman continues to hold the centre of the marketing stage, because selling is and will remain, predominantly a matter of human persuasion.

340. Ultimate Sale: Key

Alexander Heron in his book "No Sale, No Job" writes, "The ultimate sale has become the measure of the success of every enterprise from the mine or farm to the travel bureau. That ultimate sale is the incentive for the discovery of oil, the efficient layout of the factory, the reduction of costs of extraction, conversion and distribution. It is the all-powerful governor of the level of profits, investments, production and employment."

New Status of a Salesman

341. Dispenser of Innovation

The salesman is the first dispenser of innovation. In Western society, consumers are perpetually seeking new products and benefits. The rate of innovation is staggering and the life cycle of products is growing shorter. In developing societies, the rate of innovation and product obsolescence is much slower.

342. Possessor of Knowledge

The salesman needs to have intimate knowledge of the needs of his customers, his products and the problems they will solve. The role of the salesman as a "knowledge person" is underscored while dealing with products necessitating sound technical know-how, e.g., pharmaceuticals, industrial products, electronics, etc.

343. Agent of Social Change

Many of the rural dwellers are not exposed to laptops, cameras, mobile phones, etc. To these villagers, the salesman ushers a better and improved mode of living. He introduces them to hygiene through soap, to convenience through a rice cooker, and to improved productivity through tractors.

344. Provider of Utilities

The marketing mix comprises of the four P's, i.e. Product, Price, Place and Promotion. The salesman converts these concepts into practice by adding utilities to the product.

345. Catalytic Agent

Goods that are produced must be purchased and consumed in increasingly larger quantities to reduce costs, generate income and wealth and create jobs. Consumption is an essential prerequisite for employment generation.

346. Company Representative

The salesman is the representative of the company for retailers and consumers. The actions, behaviour, attitude, bearing of the salesman are inputs in the minds of the consumers and the trade. He is at once the generator and the guardian of the company's interests, repute and goodwill.

347. Intelligence Agent

In large countries like India, China, etc., communication between the market and the manufacturer is critical. In an inflationary situation when discretionary incomes are squeezed, the attitudes and actions of consumers are difficult to predict. Therefore, ideas and feedback have yet to flow from salesmen to the company.

348. A Service Provider

A sale is a "solution to a problem". A buyer is not interested in a product but a solution to his problem. A salesman, who carries a solution before entering an outlet, carries an order out. Selling is based on the principle of customer satisfaction. The consumer buys the services and the reputation of the salesman and the company.

349. Social Obligations

The increased emphasis on the social obligations of business has underscored the trade and social responsibilities of the salesman, who is the company's live contact with the customer. There is a spate of new legislation regarding pricing, packaging, weights and measurements, etc. A key task of the salesman is to educate the retailers about these legislative acts.

350. Haircut and Corporate Impressions

Across countries and continents, I have stopped market work, when salesmen were not well turned out. In one instance, I stopped the market operation and sent a salesman for a haircut and shave. In another instance, I stopped work, so that a salesman could get his shoes polished before commencing his calls again.

351. Salesman and Marketing Concept

Within companies, the salesman is an important element in the new marketing concept, which governs the thinking of top management. If product planning has roots in intimate knowledge of the consumer, then the individual salesman is in a cardinal position to communicate consumer needs to the company.

352. Salesman: Honest Guide

The salesman who could sell a refrigerator to the Eskimo is no longer esteemed. Instead, he should persuade the bizarre Eskimo who wants a refrigerator, not to buy it. However, more is expected of the salesman. He should educate the Eskimo on the benefits of a warm heater and arrange it for him.

353. Motivating the Salesman

The salesman has to be kept motivated through financial incentives and honest human relations. Salesmen with potential should be identified and promoted to the management cadres. Smart companies reward their field forces with stock options, so that they have a long-term stake in the organisation.

354. Saint Mother Teresa, Break Bread

Saint Mother Teresa said that, "A family that eats together stays together!" It is important to break bread with your team members.

355. Salesman: Pillar of Free Society

The salesperson is the pillar of a free society. Freedom means a choice among alternatives. Freedom to choose also implies the freedom to persuade others to a certain course of action or behaviour. The salesman is thus a dynamic symbol of a free society.

356. Salesmen and Soldiers

The basic armour of the soldier and the salesperson is the same: Courage, an indefatigable will to win and the guts to defy defeat.

* * *

A provident step for many retailers and local governments would be, to set up retail centres, a few kilometres outside the main town. These shopping and retail centres, could house large plus small retail formats, with food courts and restaurants, ringed by gardens, parks and recreational facilities. A good example of this is Wrentham Village outlets, about 45 minutes from Boston. The complex houses some of the best global brands e.g. Burberry, Calvin Klein, Hugo Boss, Kenneth Cole, Saks Fifth Avenue, etc.

* * *

8

Revolution In Modern Retailing

A silent revolution in retailing is underway. Consumers are willing to spend more for a pleasurable shopping experience. They are often willing to spend, instead of saving. The factors accelerating the change in shopping habits are higher incomes, convenience, need for better experiences, globalisation of market, etc.

357. Higher Disposable Incomes

We live in a richer world. Generally, the middle and upper classes, across the world, are richer than they were, three decades ago. The middle classes have decent jobs, bank balances and homes.

358. Convenience of One Roof

A shopping mall is designed for your family and you to enjoy a range of conveniences, under a single roof.

359. Shopping: An Exhilarating Experience

A visit to a shopping mall or a hypermarket has to uplift your family and you. It is like seeing a great painting. The quantum of time, energy and money spent in designing malls and supermarkets, their zones, outlets, defies imagination. The goal: to make your visit so gratifying and terrific that you visit the mall repeatedly.

360. Globalisation of Markets

The fluidity of borders between countries has made it easier for products to travel. A mall in the Middle East offers all the brands marketed in the USA or Europe, frequently, at cheaper prices. The revolution in packaging has accelerated the globalisation of brands.

361. Anti-Incumbency Vote

The success of malls and supermarkets is also an anti-incumbency vote, against conventional "bazaars" or "souks" retailing. Shoppers just got glum with jumbled outlets, untidy streets or shops, etc. The balance of power, as has happened in the USA and Europe, will shift from manufacturers to retailers.

Retail Dilemmas, Developing Countries

362. Open Doors, for FDI

It is time to review the restrictions on foreign investment by multi-brand retailers, which prevents global retailers from opening stores and providing consumers with a refreshing shopping experience. Opening the markets to global retailers has the potential to provide enormous opportunities for small businesses, through local sourcing and sharing of new technologies.

363. Infrastructural Support

Many malls could do better with improved infrastructure around them and within too. The roads leading to the mall are frequently clogged with traffic. Malls could improve their clustering. A food outlet should not be next to a shoe store. Many shopping zones and malls ignore the basic principle of "cohesive clusters", whereby affiliated outlets are bunched together.

364. Real Estate Prices, Rentals

Perhaps the pivotal reason for the tardy progress of the retail sector is the high real estate prices and rentals prevailing in most cities, in India. Thus, many retail projects are launched at available spaces, rather than at optimum catchment locations.

365. Sizes of Outlets

Due to the exorbitant real estate prices, many retail concepts, compromise on the size of the outlets. Some of the modern trade grocery outlets in the metro cities that sell groceries, vegetables and fruits, are too small. Many retail concepts often have to compromise on areas like staff recreation, canteens and toilet areas due to the tight space and high real estate prices and rentals.

366. Develop Retail Centres, Townships

A provident step for many retailers and local governments would be, to set up retail centres, a few kilometres outside the main town. These shopping and retail centres, could house large plus small retail formats, with food courts and restaurants, ringed by gardens, parks and recreational facilities. A good example of this is Wrentham Village outlets, about 45 minutes from Boston. The complex houses some of the best global brands e.g. Burberry, Calvin Klein, Hugo Boss, Kenneth Cole, Saks Fifth Avenue, etc.

367. Develop Staff

Retail staff should receive intensive training and development. Product knowledge should be emphasised. Floor staff needs to be trained in the value of a simple "smile"!

368. Aesthetics – Look Good, Feel Good

Retailers will benefit from attention to aesthetics and presentation of outlets. Shopping zones and malls should have a theme. Architectural beauty and differentiation can augment sales.

369. Retailing Is Work

Finally, retailing is rigorous work.

Advantages: Organised Retail

370. Lower Consumer Prices

Supermarkets offer better prices to the consumers. They buy in bulk, and are able to negotiate better prices from the farmers and suppliers. Since the market is very competitive, such savings are normally passed on to consumers.

371. Good Quality

Consumers are assured of good quality products. Hypermarkets clean and grade their wares like fruits and vegetables to merchandise them. In many developing countries, fruits and vegetables are frequently sold on open pavements and are often coated with dust.

372. Staff Have Careers

Staff who work in hypermarkets and supermarkets undergo regular training and development, which enhances their skills. If the staff working in such stores perform well, they can have careers in retailing i.e. literally graduate from floor salesmen to store managers.

373. Socially Responsible

Supermarkets follow socially responsible policies. Marks & Spencer follow very sensible policies. When they select a new supplier, they first check the facilities like restrooms, canteens, etc., for the staff. Only if the supplier clears this critical test, they proceed further.

374. Partnerships with Vendors

Enlightened retailers and supermarkets partner with their vendors. They collaborate to improve the basic product itself. For instance, the McDonald's Research Centre works with farmers, to upgrade the quality of the potatoes they use for their French fries.

375. Positive Approach Needed

Developing countries should refrain from politicising the arrival of organised retail. Even Russia and China have principally turned fashionably capitalist and welcomed hypermarkets and Western brands with musical bands at the airports.

376. Supermarkets, Groceries Coexist

In many second world countries like Indonesia, Brazil, Venezuela, Colombia, Saudi Arabia, etc. where international hypermarkets contribute around 50 per cent of the trade, the balance half of the business yet takes place through the traditional corner stores or small grocers.

377. Retail Foreign Direct Investment

Permitting Foreign Direct Investment (FDI) in multi-branded Retail will encourage large retailers like Metro, Tesco, Carrefour, etc. to view developing countries favourably as an investment destination. The entry of these international players ushers new paradigms in retailing.

378. Rising Costs of Retail

A rise in costs of real estate is a pure function of the demand and supply equation. Retailers will expand their operations beyond the existing city limits and borders. A large hypermarket would need 1,00,000 to 2,00,000 square feet for a good quality outlet.

379. Locating Large New Hypermarkets

It would be smart to position large hypermarkets outside the cities, where the land and rentals are cheaper. These hypermarket concepts come with restaurants, etc., and would become weekend shopping destinations.

380. Developers Will Gain

The real estate and mall developers will also gain from appreciation in their assets' prices. These builders and investors are investing their moneys in buildings and retail concepts on the basis of their faith in the consumers and the future. So, if they become rich, they deserve to.

Managing Profitable Retail

381. Site, Site and Site

The most critical success factor in retailing is the location or the site. In the mall shoppers tend to frequent the ground and first floors. Availability of escalators can augment the flow of shoppers, on the higher floors.

382. Product Concept, Merchandise

Why do consumers flock to Zara, Paris Gallery, Marks & Spencer, Virgin and H&M? These stores offer concepts. They offer solutions, not merely a trouser or a handbag. They offer style, status and class. Customers have to be constantly tantalised with new experiences.

383. Customer-Service

Successful stores have alert, energetic staff who listen and assist. Many retail outlets across developing countries score poorly on Customer-Service. Their staff need training. They may have long working hours, inadequate breaks and mingy arrangements for refreshments.

384. Visibility in Stores

Customers believe what they see. Merchandise that is aesthetically displayed draws shoppers. Retailers employ professional architects, designers and visualisers to make the store appealing. The product must scream: "Take me home. Now!"

385. After Sales Service

Every sale is a "relationship" with a customer. The sale does not end with the cash memo bring printed. It begins. The sale is successful if the customer returns to the store. The staff should respect the customer even after the billing. Stores should be very concerned about unhappy customers.

386. Customer Loyalty Programmes

A sure way to build customer faithfulness is to have a loyalty programme, which offers incentives to consumers on achieving certain milestones. Customers who enrol in these loyalty programmes, become an extended family of the store.

387. Food and Drinks, Please!

Visits to shopping malls are becoming half to full day expeditions, due to inordinate transit times and parking delays. Moreover, in the mall itself, people tend to walk and walk. So, they feel thirsty and hungry. A customer should not have to walk more than 5 to 10 minutes to get refreshments.

388. Customer Help Desks

Malls are growing massive. Some of them are becoming small townships by themselves in the Middle East, South Africa and Latin America. Malls offer shopping, five-star, hotels, restaurant facilities and gymnasiums. Anyone can get lost in these five to seven star extravaganzas. Malls have to be user-friendly.

389. Entertainment

Retailers have to dance ceaselessly, to magnetise customers. Retail outlets will have sales promotions, kids' competitions, music, pianists and violinists, to ensure that customers flock to them. Malls organise carnivals, fashion shows, shopping festivals to lure customers.

390. Ringing Cash Register: Music!

Various facilities should interweave, to lure customers, just as in an orchestra, music from all the instruments has to blend to make harmonious music. For the successful retailer, ringing cash registers make the most melodious music!

391. Parking Space

Most malls tend to provide parking space from 1,000 to 6,000 cars, depending on its size. In Sao Paulo, new malls devote three to four floors of the mall to parking space. In retailing, every square foot can generate revenue, money and profit; so some malls regretfully neglect parking.

Launching a New Retail Brand

392. First parameter - Four Ps

Audit the launch package on the anvil of the Four P's of marketing i.e. Product, Price, Place and Promotion.

393. Product

The retailer must think through the store to be launched, its value proposition, the positioning, its ingredients, segment of consumers being catered to and the packaging or appearance of the store.

394. Price

Pricing will be determined by the positioning in the market and competitor prices.

395. Place

The retailer has to decide, should the product be sold in top-class malls or in the High Street outlets or both.

396. Promotions and Advertising

This covers advertising media like the television, radio, newspapers, magazines, etc. and in-shop activities, sampling, etc.

397. Top Class Team

Select a top-class, competent team to launch the product concept. Focus on building and buying the best team, within the budget. Good professionals are expensive, but they deliver success.

398. New Paradigms

Think outside the box or normal paradigms. Retailers should read evolving markets rapidly, to comprehend new trends, patterns and fashions.

399. Clear, Quantifiable Goals

Determine clear goals for at least three to five years prior to launching a new retail brand. Metrics that can be used for defining the goals of a new launch are: 1) Market share, 2) Profit contribution, 3) Sales turnover and 4) Volumes in quantity terms.

400. Summary

Smart retailers when launching new brands, will ensure that they audit the entire marketing package on the anvil of the Four Ps of marketing, recruit the best teams that money can buy, recognise Emerging Consumer Segments and have quantifiable goals for at least five years.

Entrepreneurial Retail Managers

401. Knowledge of Market

Entrepreneurial Retail managers would have profound knowledge of consumers, trading patterns and wholesale markets. Retailing has to be highly supply chain oriented. Rigorous knowledge of trading patterns and middlemen behaviour is crucial to becoming a successful retailer.

402. Defeat-Busters

These Entrepreneurial Retail Managers are principally self-driven, set ambitious personal and corporate goals. They take strong risks to progress the business and their own careers. They would be managers, who do not give up, ever. They defy defeat. Retail is fiercely competitive. Walmart, Carrefour, Tesco, etc., compete agonisingly, for every cent. Tough negotiators should head retail businesses.

403. Visionaries

Entrepreneurial managers would be visionaries who would be capable of strong action. They operate beyond traditional boundaries and spot new opportunities, markets and successes. They buffer beliefs with courageous action.

404. Mid-Career Professionals

Entrepreneurial managers would be mid-career professionals, with 15 to 20 years' experience. These professionals would have a track record of overcoming adversities i.e. delivering in tough markets, defeating established competitors and building robust teams. They would be men who have turned defeats into successes.

405. "Mavericks"

Entrepreneurial retail managers may not fit in conventional descriptions. They could have been classified as "cranks", "unconventional" and "bizarre" at a selection. However, if we are searching for leaders, who redraw maps, we will need entrepreneurs who challenge normal classifications. They would typically command fierce loyalty from their teams.

406. "Mercenary Breed"

These entrepreneurial managers may not be outstandingly loyal to the organisations they work for, in terms of long-term careers. However, they would be ruthlessly professional in their dealings e.g. confidentiality, ethics, etc. There is an emerging breed of managers, whose professional careers are from contract to contract. Driven by professional egos, they build strong teams.

Finding Entrepreneurial Managers

407. Within the Retail Business

Most companies would have 10 to 15 per cent of its managers in this entrepreneurial category. Examine the career paths of managers who may have been on the "High Potential" bandwagon, but then disembarked due to some mishap. They may have tucked away their troubles and are raring to go again. It is an embattled Prime Minister Winston Churchill or a rugged General George Patton that we seek.

408. Poaching

Retail will also need to poach aggressively from other retail companies all over the world. Study successful retail groups, concepts; probe the leaders who are responsible for these accomplishments and lure them by offering them challenges and opportunities.

409. Train Young Managers

Retail should inculcate entrepreneurial values among younger managers, through training programs, to ensure percolation of a restless, searching spirit among potential leaders. Their role models have to be Bill Gates, Sam Walton and David Sainsbury.

Reward Entrepreneurial Managers

410. Give them Space

Strong and able retail leaders need space and freedom, to build teams and deliver results. Their jobs are frequently unstructured; they have to introduce new systems and processes. If anyone breathes down their neck, they rebel.

411. Let Leaders Deliver

Leaders need to be left alone sometimes, to deliver.

412. Pay More than Market

These entrepreneurial managers have to be paid competitively. Change agents are risk-intoxicated. Failure is expensive for them in terms of credibility and career. Correspondingly, success should ensure gorgeous rewards for them to be motivated. Monetary rewards could motivate entrepreneurial managers to raise the bar after each lap.

413. Immediate Returns

These managers prefer high immediate rewards, i.e. cash bonuses and stock options as compared to retirement benefits. These entrepreneurial managers could be receiving cash bonuses up to 100 per cent or more of their annual salaries, for turning around a business.

Energise Entrepreneurial Managers

414. Back to the Drawing Board

Retail companies should review whether operating environments and reward systems foster the entrepreneurial manager. Excessive regimentation should not curb creativity, which is a staple spur in an entrepreneur.

415. Rewarding and Retaining them

High monetary rewards and faster rises to tougher jobs, are the keys to rewarding and retaining entrepreneurial managers.

416. Financial Trophies

For such entrepreneurial managers, the best reward is an even tougher job! However, unless the retail group is growing rapidly, it may not be possible to keep adding to the responsibilities of such managers. Then, financial trophies, i.e. bonuses and profit-sharing schemes, can motivate them. Smart retail organisations, will have profit sharing schemes for their CEOs.

417. Chairman's Challenge

The challenge for retail will be to evolve organisational structures and cultures to be market leaders and yet rejoice entrepreneurship and individual initiative at all levels. That will be the key challenge for the retail Chairman.

Future of High-Streets Malls

418. High Streets Losing Lustre?

Since High Streets evolve with time, there is no specific pattern in their layout. A tailor could be located next to a branded apparel shop or a footwear outlet next to a restaurant. Nevertheless, there could also be a dozen outlets selling the same or similar products, because the first was a success.

419. Parking: What Is That?

The biggest threat to High Street shopping is the absence of parking space. Most urban middle class families now own a minimum of two cars. We have forgotten to walk. Shoppers park their cars a few kilometres away and then either taxi to the shops or walk there.

420. Poor to Weak Security

High Street shopping is also endangered by security concerns in some cities. There is a higher possibility of pickpockets operating in the streets, than in shopping malls. Police officers do protect the High Streets; however malls have elaborate security systems, cameras and personnel.

421. Food and the Games?

Shopping is becoming a family activity. High Streets offer a circumscribed range of options for the family. In a mall, mummy shops, the children are at a play centre, the teenagers watch a movie and papa sips coffee. The High Street does not offer so many options.

422. Remember the Basics!

Try finding a toilet after a few hours of shopping, in Oxford Street, London. The best chance is to visit a McDonald's. Or, if you are weary of walking the shops at Rua Bela Cintra in Sao Paulo, find a bench to rest your legs. Again, your best bet would be a coffee shop. High Streets do not have as many toilets, coffee shops, and customer facilities, as the malls do.

423. High Street Food yet Reigns!

Significantly, High Streets offering food, have managed to neutralise the onslaught of malls and food courts. The range of open-air cafes and restaurants at Al Diyafa in Dubai, allures hundreds of families every evening. The restaurants opposite BurJuman Centre, Dubai, attract customers every hour.

424. It Is the Rentals, Really!

The tussle of deciding whether to set up a concept in a mall or the High Street, will depend significantly on the rentals in these areas and the expected revenues per square foot. If the rentals in the malls are very high, retailers will be compelled to move to the High Street, where rentals may be modest.

425. Competition and High Streets

The competition from shopping malls will spur High Street outlets, to improved presentation and modernisation of their outlets. High Street shopping will have to budget more options and facilities if they wish to compete with the malls in the future.

426. Mall Offerings

The malls will offer a range of services, which the High Streets will find it difficult to match, in the short run. For instance, the Al Futtaim City Centre Mall, in Muscat, (population less than a million), offers its shoppers about 150 fashion and contemporary retail outlets. To make the shoppers comfortable, the mall offers wheelchairs to the elderly and infirm at no extra cost, complimentary baby carts, pay phones, an Information Desk, Mall gift vouchers of required denominations, etc.

427. Prayer Rooms, Too

The Muscat Mall further offers separate prayer rooms for men and women, baby changing rooms, restrooms across the mall, special restrooms for the disabled, ATM booths of five banks, with one bank offering full-fledged banking services, multi-level parking for 2,250 cars and regular taxi services. It also offers valet services.

428. Dubai Mall - A Town

The Dubai Mall in the UAE has raised the expectations of consumers even further, with its facilities. The site area was in excess of 12.1 million square feet. The structural steel used in the mall, was double than that deployed in the Eiffel Tower, i.e. 7,300 tonnes. The net leasable area is equal to area of 50 football fields, strung together. The mall houses around 1,200 retail outlets. It has a gold market with 220 retailers. It has the world's largest indoor aquarium, with 33,000 living animals including sharks. A tunnel runs through the tank, holding 10 million litres of water. There is parking for 14,000 cars and a five-star hotel with 700 rooms.

429. Mall, A Town

Now, how can any High Street compete with a mall, which is a town by itself? A visitor to Dubai can stay in the hotel next to Dubai Mall and just stay put there, since all the shopping and recreational options are available under one roof.

430. Coexistence Possible

Brazil has exclusive malls for sales of furniture. Dubai has branded electronics outlets of over 1,00,000 square feet each. Saudi Arabia has exclusive 50,000 square feet outlets, selling only books and stationery. High Street shopping will also flourish, depending on the products being sold, the status attached to the street and the segment of the market being catered to. There will be coexistence, perhaps even some congruence, between the malls and High Street shopping in the future.

431. High Street Improvements

The arrival of mall culture will definitely depress some sales in the High Streets. High Street outlets will have to spruce and energise themselves to meet the sharper competition from the malls. The mall culture will also improve Customer-Service in the High Street.

432. High Streets, Think Laterally!!

Lateral thinking, generating unique new paradigms, could benefit High Street retailers. For instance: No visit to London is complete without a walk on Oxford street, i.e. from Marble Arch to Oxford Circus stations. Many popular fashion brands are housed in this High Street, between these two metro rail stations. So why not think of a totally innovative solution of a transparent glass roof, covering the entire street, banning all traffic on the road, and transforming it into a mall?

433. Prisons as Malls in Brazil

In towns like Fortaleza and Salvador in Brazil, if you need to buy local handicrafts, paintings, embroidered tablecloths, laced dresses, etc., you normally visit a single storied building, in a compound. Each outlet is installed in a single room-type shop. Each shop leads into another. I was so intrigued by these cute markets that I enquired of my colleagues, how they evolved. The reply flummoxed me. These building were prisons many years ago!

434. Necessity Generates Inventions

As crime rates declined, the prisons were no longer required. The authorities converted these prisons into markets for arts and handicrafts! Each shop in a room had earlier been a cell for prisoners. Thus, necessity is the mother of all invention. Opportunities for retail are boundless. We merely have to spot them and build on them.

435. "Market-Malls", Uruguay

In Montevideo, the capital of Uruguay, some of the street markets, are already clustered in predesigned formats and have transparent dome-like circular ceilings, which give them an appearance of being malls. These High Street "market-malls", will never be threatened by any retail concept. Youngsters flock here every night to sip champagne and beer till the wee hours of the morning.

436. Diversification in to New Markets

The preponderance of malls or specialised retail concepts can also lead to a changed sales and marketing strategy amongst High Street retail outlets. A decade ago, anyone in Dubai, who wanted to buy a laptop or a desktop computer, headed straight to Computer Street. However, the arrival of electronics retailers like "Jumbo", "Plug Ins", "Sharaf DG", etc., changed the computer market paradigm in Dubai.

437. More Elegance Please!

In developing shopping malls, we should aim to build theme malls, which are exquisite and architecturally innovative, so that shopping in them is a real delight. A classic example of themed mall concept is the Ibn Battuta Mall in Dubai.

438. Human Relations in Retail

Ten Critical Success Factors for Great Human Relations Management are (1) Build Corporate Passion, (2) Respect the Sales Floors, (3) Do Not Forget Grooming, (4) Training and Development, (5) Do Not Lose Your Jewels, (6) Building Careers, (7) Stock Options to All, (8) The Basics, (9) Welcome Unions, and (10) Dance Sometimes.

439. Build Corporate Passion

The first ingredient of flourishing human relations in retail management is to imbibe a passion for success amongst the employees. Staff should be enthused by the corporate mission. Organisations succeed, not merely when the directors are motivated, but when every employee down the line, i.e. the packer or the security guard, are fully charged by the same mission.

440. Respect the Sales Floors

An astute retailer will walk the floors of the store every day. In a Customer-Service oriented retail outlet, the supervisory staff, whether managers or directors or the chairman of the company, will walk the floors. They will talk to the staff, about their families, their health, transport facilities and only then about their products. They will seek advice, views and customer responses, from their floor sales staff.

441. Do Not Forget Grooming!!

Retailing is about the staff donning clean and well-pressed uniforms. It is about shaving daily. It is about using the right type and quantum of deodorant. Retailing is also about bright enthusiastic eyes and warm smiles. It is about polished shoes. These are fundamental factors, but they make or break a sale.

442. Training and Development

Each employee would spend at least 10 working days per annum, in classroom training. Training has to be constant and ceaseless, in the classroom and on the floors on a daily ongoing basis.

443. Do Not Lose Your Jewels!!

Talent and skill are scarce. It is always sensible to retain quality staff. It takes decades, to inculcate the team with corporate values and a certain "way of doing business". It tests nerves to train managers. The people, who work in the store, are the jewels of the company. A smart retailer will value his human resources. Happy teams, generate profits.

444. Building Careers

It is vital to build careers and promote people from within the company. Internal progression systems augment loyalty and boost morale. The staff is strongly motivated by the belief that they will grow, when they deliver results.

445. Stock Options to All

Retailers would do well to make every employee a partner, through stock options or a profit sharing scheme. It would be provident to evolve a scheme to place the entire team, including the packing man, on a salary and stock options remuneration system. A watchman, who knows that he has a stake in the final profits, will ensure zero levels of shrinkage.

446. Treatment and Training

Astute retailers will look after the health and wellbeing of their staff, providing good meals, washrooms and restrooms. They will train them continuously, and they will motivate them not just with money, but also with respect, a career path and a sense that they are part of a family.

Staff training is a retailer's best investment. Retailers have to accept the fact that skills are scarce. Even when the talent pool is large, it always makes sense to retain good staff.

447. The Basics

Store managers will have to play the role of entrepreneurs and businessmen. Motivating personnel will require providing basic hygiene factors for all personnel. It is crucial to provide restrooms, canteens, dining areas and recreation rooms to the staff. A retailer will earn a lot of revenue per square foot, when those who are responsible for generating it are well treated.

448. Welcome Unions

Unions are a reality and should be welcomed. They are the collective voice of the employees, the partners in the enterprise. Unions are constructive when the relationships between the employers and employees are fair. It is best to treat their workers humanely and fairly.

449. Dance Sometimes

Working in any company should be fun and rejuvenating. The staff should look forward eagerly to coming to work daily. This is possible, when the team also spends informal times together. If the employees of a retail company dance, sing, eat and rejoice together, the company stays together.

A, B, C, of Human Relations in Retail

450. A: Accept

Accept genuinely, that "Business is people" and retail is about dealing with people i.e. customers, suppliers and ultimately, employees. Employees are the first customers of any retail business.

451. B: Behaviour

Behaviour of the managers should demonstrate conviction of the people factor in retail management. Mission statements and words must be supported by action. Talent is desperately short in the world, and will continue to be so. So, we must respect and covet our people.

452. C: Customer-Service

Customer-Service is the soul of any retail outlet. If all the employees comprehend and believe in this concept passionately, the outlet will be the "talk of the town". Any retail outlet, ultimately sells, services and smiles.

453. D: Develop

Develop leaders, everywhere! There is a leader in every sales girl, merchandiser or manager. (In a recent Hindi movie, a character pronounces, "There is a lion in everyone. It only needs someone to tickle it, to make it roar!"). Leadership qualities can be developed amongst team members through on-the-job training, classroom training and also counselling sessions.

454. E: Establish

Establish systems, manuals, procedures and business processes for all retail operations in rigorous detail. Manuals also prescribe procedures, for standardisation of fundamentals across retail stores and branches. Lest we forget: Retail is Detail!

455. F: Forge

Forge teams out of employees. Make each section, floor, category an independent unit, and foster team spirit by giving them collective tasks and team prizes for achievements. Encourage the teams to spend informal times together i.e. a picnic, movie or outing, to augment bonding.

456. G: Generate

Generate challenges to keep your high-fliers motoring in top gear. These high performance managers, need to kill a lion daily (i.e. manage a challenge daily). High performance staff has to be kept ceaselessly motivated through innovative concepts, ideas, rapid expansions and diversifications.

457. H: Help

Help your employees round the clock. If someone falls sick in the middle of the night, train your managers to land up at the employee's house to take him to the hospital or look after him. Dedicated and devoted teams are the result of the mind-set of being a "Help-Desk" to your employees.

458. I: Involve

Involve your top management in key decisions pertaining to new concepts, expansions, diversifications and promotions of senior staff.

459. J: Judge

Judge employees on pure merit. Retailers, who run their businesses professionally, flourish. Avoid favouritism and nepotism like the plague. In a family business make your sons and daughters labour their way, up the ladder, like a trainee. You will then teach them the best lessons of their lives.

460. K: Knowledge

Knowledge is power in the retail business. Product knowledge is the key to excellent Customer-Service. Employees should be updated constantly on new technologies, IT systems, selling techniques, etc.

461. L: Losing

Losing a retail professional or team, built over the years, due to petty squabbling, ego-clashes or feeble remuneration, is unwise. Ordinary people, who work selflessly in a store, are the foundation of great retail businesses.

462. M: Motivate

Motivate teams for superior performance through personal encouragement, financial rewards, status enhancement, sales contests, bonuses, so that teams feel invigorated and appreciated.

463. N: Niceties

Niceties are important. Never ever condone the use of foul language or uncouth manners on the shop floors. Chewing of gum, winking, scratching, talking on the mobile, etc., is highly obnoxious to customers.

464. O: Outperform

"Outperform targets" culture! Encourage your team, so that they do not just meet targets, but exceed them. Teams must be willing to take that little incremental walk, that extra mile to meet goals.

465. P: Profits

Profits are crucial to a retail business. Without profits, no business can survive. However, profits augment if the habit of thinking profits is inculcated down the line. Directors, managers, staff or watchmen must all think profits.

466. Q: Quiet

Quiet periods, whereby senior managers get away from the daily store pressures, once a quarter, help to generate new ideas. So, have a "blue-sky" day, debating innovations and improvements.

467. R: Remunerating

Remunerating the team judiciously is a key element of retailing. If a retailer pays employees below their market value, they will depart. It takes time and money to recruit and train new staff.

468. S: Salary

Salary reviews, comparisons with competitors are vital to ensure that staff is remunerated competitively. This will also contribute to retaining the team.

469. T: Training

Training and development of the staff on a continuous basis, brings latest management practices into the retail group and also motivates the staff. Top team members must be sensitised to dealing with the government and local authorities.

470. U: Understand

Understand the customers, via the floor staff, by spending time with them in the shops. Sales staffs on the floors are brilliant sources of information about customer preferences. These insights are free.

471. V: Very

Very important it is, for top management to interact with the Governments to explicate the advantages of large formats of retail for employment generation and tax revenues.

472. W: Wee Benefits

Extra benefits like a meal scheme, transportation from and to the residence, when the workplace is far away, make a massive difference to the morale of a team at negligible costs.

473. X: X-Rayable

X-rayable transparent operations, invariably ensure respect from employees. A transparently managed retail business, that pays taxes, adheres to labour laws, pays its employees on time and stands glued to its word, lures the best talent.

474. Y: Yours

Yours is the whole retail world, if you can adhere to this list, build a team, which respects the values enshrined in the ethical practices of the company.

475. Z: Zebra

Zebra Crossing Line: The personal life of employees is akin to a Zebra crossing line in HR. Frequently employers have a habit of getting embroiled in the personal lives of their employees, which is avoidable.

Harvesting Rural Retail

476. Rural Revolution

With the gradual expansion of the Modern Retail many retailers have started eyeballing the villages for launching the self-service concepts of shopping. The entry of Modern Retail formats in the rural areas will also revolutionise shopping habits and create massive employment.

477. Importance of Rural Markets

Rural consumers are undergoing a major metamorphosis in their buying habits and consumption patterns due to improvements in living conditions. Villages will not be villages, any more, in the next few decades, in terms of consumption habits. They will commence merging into small town-urban buying habits.

478. Characteristics of Rural Consumers

Retailers planning self-service format stores in the villages, need to understand the characteristics and behaviour of rural consumers.

479. Quality Of Life

Increased incomes and improved awareness levels have made the villager seek a better quality of life. The rural consumer now demands a wider range of consumer durables and non-durables.

480. Role of Women

The influx of consumer products in the villages has highlighted the role of the rural housewife. She has now become a key influencer and decision maker in all buying decisions. The rural housewife increasingly makes up her own mind about what she will buy for her family. The literacy rate among women in the villages is improving steadily.

481. Potential for Organised Retail

With augmented awareness levels, higher income levels and rising aspirations, the rural consumer is also a target for organised retail. The rural farmer or his wife would relish a shopping experience that offers more options, variety and some pleasure.

Factors Impacting Rural Retail

482. Population Strata - Feeder markets

Organised retail should focus on markets, which are traditionally a fulcrum for wholesalers to supply products to rural retailers in surrounding villages. A small feeder market could have a population of around 50,000, but the larger feeder markets, could have a population of 500,000. Feeder markets allure customers from 100 to 250 surrounding villages. They will sustain a Modern Retail store.

483. Type of Products

The products which will enjoy high acceptability in the rural areas are:

a) Agricultural inputs like, seeds, fertilisers, pesticides, etc.,
b) Agricultural machinery and implements, for farming,
c) Transport equipment like tractors, two-wheelers, etc.

The product range will depend on the local demand. A successful chain of supermarkets in Cote d'Ivoire, sells premium perfumes and designer apparel in the urban areas in the capital Abidjan. However, in the upcountry rural markets of Bouake, it even sells live cocks and hens.

484. Politics and Retail

The politics of organised retail will be short-lived.

485. Guidelines to Entry

a) Invest for the long term,
b) Carry local community,
c) Keep the outlets spacious,
d) Train your talent,
e) Harvest rigorously, before expanding.

486. Infrastructural Impediments

a) Weak road networks,
b) Power supply,
c) Water shortages,
d) Warehousing and logistics bottlenecks,
e) Availability of suitable manpower.

487. One Last Point – Execution

Seamless execution is the soul of any business success. It is not very difficult to conceptualise new business models and paradigms. However, success depends on brilliant execution.

Business of Fashion

488. Black Is Beautiful. Ever, Forever!

Yes, black continues internationally to be the most solid and popular colour. Whilst it is commendable for formals in cold countries, it is certainly not optimum for tropical countries. Greys and browns, would be great in Singapore or Brazil. An entire industry has sprung up in black colour, at the cost of other colours.

489. Distress Look Is Great!

It is common for the rich and famous to dress up in tattered clothes. Perhaps they are tired of being wealthy and wish to peek at their roots. Torn jeans, soiled, shrunk T-shirts and socks with holes are some of the arsenal of this fashion fraternity.

490. Dressing Down Is Good?

Professionals turn up for important meetings, in casual clothes like jeans. Their shirts hang outside the trousers. The casual look is designed to be "cool", whatever that means. Dressing down may be fine when you visit your in-laws over the weekend, but not when you are bidding for a new account or if you are the President or Prime Minister of a country.

491. Designer Bags Are a Must

Every few months, brands like Gucci and Louis Vuitton launch a new handbag in limited numbers, designed to make the famous seek these pieces. Then every fashion queen of the world will seek the bag! There is status and pride in possessing the latest Gucci handbag.

492. Accessories Are You

Fine accessories made from gold, platinum, silver, combined with precious and semi-precious stones and costume accessories made from low cost materials like metals with gold or silver finishes, wood, plastic and beads will continue to sway women. Costume jewellery is usually a combination of glass, synthetic or some semi-precious stones.

493. Tight Fit, Wrap Around the Body

Fashion gurus advise avoidance of loose fit apparel, which are baggy and could make the wearer look sloppy. The perfect fit and look, is in. Sure, clothes that wrap around the body are ideal. However, for people with large waists, it would make sense to wear trousers with pleats, or a double-breasted blazer, than a single-breasted one. What about a lady with rather large hips? A loose skirt would be more appropriate for her than a tight trouser.

494. Your Style and Clothes Talk

It is better to be stylish and well dressed, than to use your wardrobe as an advertising hoarding. The most stylish jeans are not the widest, narrowest, hip hugging or rinsed; they are the ones that fit best. To the lady with substance, whilst her hair style is important, it does not matter if it is the Bob, Razor Cut with Layers, Masculine, Soft Wedge Haircut, or Poker Straight.

495. Man and Woman Stuff

The unisex sunglass or belt is the product of the laziness of the designer. Fundamentally, men prefer strong designs and metallic colours. Women lean towards more colourful, softer designs and patterns. It is better to design fashion along these traditional lines, rather than creating indistinguishable merchandise.

496. Bold Is Beautiful

Fashion is fundamentally about being comfortable with what you enjoy wearing, what makes you feel good. Eventually fashion is not merely about being different or standing out. It is about being yourself.

* * *

It is a universally acknowledged truth that human beings aspire for better living conditions and economic prosperity. In the future, consumer products will emerge as the great levellers of economic prosperity, between the rural and urban areas.

* * *

9

Revolution In Global Rural Markets

Comprehend Rural Markets

497. Rural Markets

Rural markets are blossoming due to improvements in agricultural productivity, dispersion of industry in rural areas, exposure to media like television and the rapid advancement of the Internet and mobile phone technologies. The exploding rural markets pose a prodigious challenge to marketers.

498. Huge, Growing Market

Increased incomes and improved awareness levels make the villager seek a better quality of life. The rural consumer demands a wider range of consumer durables and non-durables. Rural housewives crave for products like stoves and pressure cookers, which make cooking for the family easier and faster. The rural housewife also desires to choose her clothes from a wider range of designs and textiles.

499. Declining Food Expenditure

Across developing countries, as rural incomes augment, the proportion of expenditure on food items declines and a higher proportion of income is spent on consumer products.

500. Break-down of Feudal Structures

The power equations in the village are changing again. The villager who owns a colour TV or a car, is now held in esteem. The influx of consumer products, especially durables, is leading to a breakdown of the caste and feudal structures, which have governed rural life, for many centuries.

501. Change in Lifestyles

The villager, like his urban counterpart, is being allured by a comfortable life. It is now becoming common to see villages with a population of 5,000 to 10,000, having 50 to 200 shops selling television sets, electric mixers, sewing machines, pressure cookers, mobile phones, etc.

502. Money and Savings

The villager is beginning to believe that he can mould his own destiny. The pursuit of money is no longer frowned at. The villager is not hiding his savings in an earthen pot, buried under the floor of his house. Today he spends his surplus income on clothes, radios and televisions.

503. Willingness to Innovate

Since the rural consumer is gradually losing his suspicion about new urban products, his willingness to innovate and experiment with new products is increasing. This is making it easier for manufacturers to get higher trial rates, during new products launches.

504. Brand-Consciousness

Rural consumers are more knowledgeable about the availability of brands. A few decades ago, a rural consumer would go to a shop and merely ask for a tablet of soap. He would use the same tablet for bathing as well as for washing his clothes. The same villager now asks for a bathing soap by its brand name.

505. Fashion Consciousness

The villager is becoming more conscious of how he or she looks and grooms. Sales of textiles are on the increase. Villagers are also buying ready-made garments like shirts, trousers, shorts and frocks for children.

506. Preference for Premium Products

The rural consumer, who has the means in agriculturally rich states, is increasingly shifting from the medium-priced popular brands to expensive premium products.

507. Role of Rural Retailer

The rural consumer has always relied sturdily on the recommendations of the rural retailer. The bond between the rural retailer and the rural consumer has always been robust. Rural retailers try to build long-term relationships with their customers.

508. Rural Wholesaler Contributions

Rural wholesalers have made major contributions to deepen and widen the distribution of consumer products and agricultural implements in the rural areas. They operate on very low margins.

509. Role of Television

The commercial services of the radio and television also help to establish consumer products in the minds of the villagers. Television will eventually take durable and non-durable products into every rural home.

510. Impact of Films and TV Serials

A film star is commonly featured in rural advertising campaigns, since an actor is the symbol of power, money, glamour and sex appeal. Films have always been a major factor influencing attitudes and lifestyles in the villages. They have also been the catalytic influences to encourage migration from the rural to the urban areas.

511. Mobile Telephones, Social Media

Villages are getting habituated to mobile telephones across the world. In a decade or so, rural markets will be saturated with smart mobile phones. Mobile phones are revolutionising communications in the villages. Rural consumers will be active on social media and networking services.

512. Political Awareness

Villagers are better informed about national affairs. Radio and television play a key role in generating awareness.

513. Desire to Urbanise

Purchases of such consumer products, gives the rural consumer a psychological feeling of being a part of the urban ethos. Thus, a large number of brands, which are popular in the towns, like Lux soap, Sony TV, Casio watches, etc., are also percolating into the villages.

514. Erosion of Suspicion

Rural dwellers have traditionally been suspicious of city-folk. This suspicion is now gradually eroding. Moreover, the villager has used a number of products like soaps, torches, transistors, etc. over the last few decades and found them adding value to his life.

515. Discriminating Consumers

Retailers in rural markets are aware that villagers are discriminating customers and will check the price of a product at several shops before making a purchase. They also insist on a price reduction, though the price could be printed on the package.

516. Female Literacy

About 83 per cent of the women in the world are now literate. The widespread availability of consumer products, has underscored the role of the rural housewife, as a dominant factor in household buying decisions.

517. Value for Money

The rural housewife demands value for every cent that she spends. She will not be duped easily, since she values the limited money that she possesses.

518. Role of Small Packs

Many villagers in Africa and Asia are yet quite poor. A retailer breaks open the bigger packs of products and sells small quantities, to meet the requirements of these villagers. Firms selling soap, detergents, tea, tooth powder, pack their products in small packs for rural markets.

519. Role of Opinion Leaders

The opinion leaders in a typical village are the "sarpanch" (chief of the village council), members of the "panchayat" (village council or governing body), the "gram-sevak" (village social worker), the schoolmaster, the doctor and the government engineer.

520. Seeing Is Believing

Rural consumers have greater faith in a product, if they actually see it in use. It is therefore useful to conduct demonstrations, with a new product to strengthen credibility. Demonstrations and propaganda operations also increase the trial rates of new products.

521. Inventory Levels

The proliferation of consumer products in the villages has led to higher inventory levels in the rural shops. Shopkeepers have had to arrange incremental funds as working capital, to fund higher purchases.

522. Retail in Rural Feeder Markets

Feeder markets are large rural markets, which feed surrounding villages. The outstanding feature of most feeder markets, is that a few major retail shops account for the bulk of the business in the market.

523. Weekly Village Markets

Most villages have a weekly market, called the "haat". Retailers from surrounding markets flock to the "haat". They spread tarpaulin sheets on the ground and display a variety of consumer products. Companies make use of the "haat" to set up festive stalls to promote new products.

"Table-Top Markets" mushroom in countless villages across the African continent.

524. Impact of Harvest

A poor crop depresses the capacity of the farmer to buy consumer products. The demand for consumer products is at a peak immediately after the crops are harvested, when the farmer is flush with money. New products should ideally be launched in the villages at this time.

525. Launch of New Products

When a new product is launched in a village, companies resort to a number of promotion tactics to ensure quick awareness. Tremendous fanfare and excitement are generated when a new product is launched in the villages.

526. Cinema Vans

Awareness about consumer products is also generated by cinema and video shows held in the village squares. Vans are equipped with cinema and video exhibition equipment and they show commercial films, interspaced with popular songs.

527. Fairs and Festivals

Manufacturers also participate in fairs and festivals to boost the sales of their products. These fairs offer opportunities to communicate information about new consumer products.

528. Role of Trademarks

Rural consumers identify a brand by its trademark or logo i.e. the picture or photograph on the packaging; a matchbox with a key printed on it is called "Chavi" (key) matches.

529. Wall Paintings

Publicity of products in villages is also achieved by painting the walls with product-message. Wall paintings are costed on a per square feet basis and are very economical and effective means of generating awareness.

530. Word-of-Mouth Publicity

While publicity media are useful, word-of-mouth recommendations frequently decide the fate of a product. Rural consumers have faith in the opinion of a person like the schoolmaster, who is often one of their kith and kin. Villagers frequently assess the performance of a product, through word-of-mouth feedback.

531. Role of Television

The commercial services of the radio and television also help to establish consumer products in the minds of the villagers. Television will eventually take products into every rural home.

532. Rate of Change

While change is taking place in the rural areas through the introduction of consumer products, the rate of change should be accelerated. The absence of a network of sturdy all-weather roads is a major handicap. The cost of distribution in rural areas is also high.

533. Health Services

One of the most conspicuous features in village chemist shops, is the abundant stock of vitamins and tonics. However poor the rural farmer is, he will deny himself and save to provide vitamins and tonics for his children.

534. Sports, Travel and Leisure

Villagers are beginning to value leisure. They spend their free time listening to the radio or watching TV. Playing sports is also becoming a favourite past time in the villages. Affluent villagers are also beginning to travel.

535. Quality-Problems

Many consumer products manufactured in small towns and marketed in the villages have scant regard for quality. Rural consumers often get duped into buying spurious products.

536. New Vitality

The future will see a tremendous exuberance in the rural markets. Rural markets will continue to grow and in some cases, at rates faster than the urban growth rates.

Harvesting Rural Markets

537. Pricing, Local Selling Patterns

Pricing in developing societies, impacts the design of the products to be launched and sold. In many African countries, laundry soaps are sold as long bar soaps, say about 12 inches in length. Shopkeepers cut the soap and sell it in small pieces, depending on the amount of money a villager has.

538. Distribution Network

The ideal rural distribution comprises of traditional wholesalers, distribution vans, cycle units and even animal carts, (camels, bullocks, mules and donkeys), depending upon the local topography. A company distributing products in the villages has to blend its distribution system with the traditional wholesale channels.

539. Rapport

Establishing rapport through language and conduct is crucial in winning the confidence of the rural consumers and retailers.

540. Segmentation

Rural markets can be segmented on the basis of population, age, sex, geography, crops, etc. It is not always possible to segment rural markets sharply on the basis of incomes, due to paucity of data, in many developing societies.

541. Pricing Strategies, Restrictions

The flexibility to deploy pricing as a tool to influence demand in rural markets is limited, in countries such as India, due to the statutory provision of printing of the maximum retail price on many packaged products. Rural markets can be tapped rigorously, by giving special discounts, in the form of differential pricing, price offs, trade offers, consumer offers, etc.

542. Packaging and Pack Sizes

Packaging for rural markets should be sturdy and robust. Products for rural markets travel long distances and the external packaging should withstand frequent handling. Moreover, considering the weak purchasing power of the economically weakest rural consumers, small pack sizes containing enough product for a day or a week, are necessary.

543. Advertising for Rural

Many companies use the same advertising for both rural and urban consumers. This is not the best policy. In an advertisement, a common appeal i.e. status, affection, care, style, etc. can be used for urban and the rural markets. However, the presentation of the appeal to a rural consumer should be substantially different from the way it is presented to the urban consumer.

544. Promotions and Special Discounts

Rural promotions should ideally be conducted during the post-harvest period, when the farmers are flush with money from the sales proceeds of their crops. Promotions should be avoided during the sowing period when the farmer is investing heavily in agricultural inputs.

545. Conservative Behaviour

Villagers are conservative in their behaviour, despite their increasing prosperity. Although, TV, mobile phones and Internet are compressing the information gap between urban and rural consumers, this harmonisation will yet need more time.

546. Low Income Levels

In the villages due to lower income levels, the demand for products of daily household use like soaps, cooking oils, detergents, etc., is at economy prices. Premium or expensive brands of these products would be sold in agriculturally prosperous areas.

Rural Consumption and Development

547. Rural Development

Enhanced availability of consumer products in rural areas augments the national output, which is an aggregation of the goods and services produced in the urban and rural areas. Distribution and consumption of these products in the rural areas generates employment and incomes.

548. Employment Generation

The introduction of consumer products in rural areas generates employment opportunities in the villages. A number of villagers have started retailing groceries. A new distributive entrepreneur is emerging in the villages.

549. Monetary Economy

The proliferation of consumer products in the villages has given an impetus to the monetary economy. The salesmen and drivers who distribute consumer products in the villages get salaries from the distributors. They spend their incomes in the villages to upgrade their living conditions e.g. improved housing construction, textiles, ready-to-wear garments, electrical gadgets, etc.

550. Investments in Villages

The economic levels, attitudes and outlook of the villagers change radically, with factories and banks opening in the villages. Employment opportunities are created for hundreds of villagers. They have a regular cash flow.

551. Improved Productivity

The Green Revolution, which led to self-sufficiency in food grains, received a major thrust through the use of fertilisers, hybrid seeds, pesticides, tractors, etc. Manufacturers of fertilisers and growth nutrients have penetrated deep into the rural areas to educate farmers on their use.

552. Banking Operations

Banking operations are an indicator of economic prosperity. Improvement in the availability of consumer products and the resultant thrust in the economic development in villages are evident from the mushrooming of the branches of banks in the villages.

553. Better Health

Improved health and hygiene awareness leads to improved productivity among the villagers. The share of rural markets in the national market for basic, over-the-counter (OTC) medicines and analgesic tablets is augmenting. The availability of medicines promotes better health in the villages.

554. Awareness and Education

Education is one of the critical determinants of the level of development of a society. The mobile phone with Internet is revolutionising the mind-sets of rural dwellers. Villages perceive the television and mobile phone as "must have" items in their lives and homes. Rural markets contribute 60 per cent of new mobile phone subscriptions, in many developing countries.

555. Improved Quality of Life

The availability of consumer products has made the lives of the villagers more comfortable and better organised. The improved availability of ready-made garments, hygienically packed foods like biscuits and time saving gadgets are enabling villagers to perform their household chores with greater ease and comfort.

556. Universal Truth

It is a universally acknowledged truth that human beings aspire for better living conditions and economic prosperity. In the future, consumer products will emerge as the great levellers of economic prosperity, between the rural and urban areas.

Launching New Products in Villages

557. Define Areas

Identify specific rural areas, in which a new product is to be launched, to focus efforts and resources in the most potential areas.

558. Crucial Role of Time

New products launches, like promotions, should ideally be during the post-harvest period.

559. Retailer Dynamics

The rural retailer is a key element in the success of a new product. He has to be convinced about the quality of a product.

560. Explain Margins Carefully

Rural retailers are heavily influenced by the margins that they will earn on the new product. Therefore, the margins on the product must be explained to the retailer.

561. Generate Quick Awareness

Companies use a variety of promotional techniques to generate quick awareness about a product in the village. A huge procession is often taken through the village, led by a band.

562. Paint the Village

To generate quick awareness and trial of the new product, it is useful to paint some important retail shops with the product message.

563. Brief Opinion Leaders

Villagers attach a lot of importance to the views of the schoolmaster, the "sarpanch" (chief of the village council) and other officials like an engineer, doctor, etc. It is useful to meet such opinion leaders in the village and brief them about the new product.

564. Focus on Quality

The rural consumer has become very fastidious about quality. Rural consumers have become extremely particular and do not get duped into buying inferior quality stocks.

565. Ensure Adequate Stocks

It is vital to ensure that there are adequate stocks of the new product in the villages, to cover the launch quantities and a round of replacement.

566. Show the Product

If a new detergent powder, is being launched, it is useful to offer to wash some clothes at the retailer's premises (however bizarre this may sound!) Win one retailer and you win a thousand customers.

567. Tell Success Stories

If the new product has already been launched and has been successful in some other villages, it will be advantageous to underscore the success story to the retailers. Nothing sells like success.

Goals of Rural Advertising

568. Role of Rural Advertising

Advertising also has a crucial role to play in boosting sales and changing the attitudes, habits and lifestyles of villagers in key social areas e.g. literacy, family planning, hygiene, education, etc.

569. Educate about Product Concepts

Rural consumers have to be introduced to and educated in the use of new product concepts, e.g. hybrid seeds, growth nutrients, pesticides, primus stoves, etc.

570. Strengthen Brand Image

Advertising may be undertaken in the villages to strengthen certain brand "images" or "features" of a brand, in the consumer's mind at periodic intervals. An already popular brand of batteries, may undertake a sustained campaign to underscore the long lasting life of the battery cell.

571. Build Brand Loyalty

Rural advertising is undertaken to build and strengthen brand loyalty among existing consumers. Such advertising emphasises the brand, the logo and even the name of the manufacturer.

572. Change Values and Attitudes

Advertising is also undertaken to change the thinking, beliefs, habits and values of the villagers. Changes in value systems and beliefs, take place over extended spans of time. Therefore, advertising which seeks to transform belief systems and attitudes has to be sustained over longer periods of time.

573. Boost Field Force Morale

Advertising is frequently deployed in the rural areas to support the selling efforts of the field force during a special sales drive. Rural advertising also boosts the morale of the field force.

574. Inform Consumers

A company may need to inform the rural consumers about the launch of a new brand, the range, numbers of variants, availability points, etc.

575. Announce Special Offers

Companies advertise in the rural areas to inform consumers about special offers like a discount or a consumer promotion like a free gift.

Rural Advertising Strategies

576. Positioning and Segmentation

Advertising in the rural areas is expensive. It is, therefore, vital to be clear about the positioning of the product and the precise segments of the rural market, at which the product is aimed. This helps to focus the advertising on the precise target audience.

577. Blend Advertising, Local Ethos

Advertising should be in harmony with the values of the villagers. Advertising which is considered appealing in the urban areas may be perceived as outlandish, in the villages.

578. Be Straightforward and Direct

The product purpose and benefit should be stated as directly as possible, in rural advertisements. This necessitates, telling what the product is and the advantages of buying it.

579. Emphasise Benefits and Results

The benefits that the villager will derive by using the product should be accentuated in the advertisement. An advertisement, which shows problem resolution, will have higher receptivity.

580. Avoid Patronising

The tendency to treat villagers, as novices must be scrupulously avoided, in the advertisements.

581. Stage of Advertising

The advertiser must be clear about the precise stage of the product, in its life cycle. Advertising can be pioneering, competitive or retentive, depending upon the product life cycle.

582. Generate Word-of-Mouth Publicity

Rural dwellers depend substantially on the recommendations and views of their friends, neighbours, relatives and retailers in deciding whether to buy a new brand. A well-constructed advertisement will generate ample positive, word-of-mouth mentions among the villagers.

583. Synchronise with Marketing

Marketing activities should coincide with the bursts of advertising to maximise sales. Companies undertake a variety of promotions in the villages, designed to augment retailer stock covers and consumer sales.

584. Timing of Rural Advertising Bursts

Purchases of consumer non-durables and durables tend to peak during the post-harvest, festival and marriage periods. Hence advertising should be concentrated during these celebration times.

585. Announcer Advertisements

Special announcer rural advertising is undertaken, for a certain time span, whenever a new product is launched. The purpose of announcer advertising is to inform the villagers about the launch of the new product, its brand name, key promise, usage benefits, etc.

586. Repeat Advertising

Repeated reiteration of the product-message is crucial in the rural markets, particularly when introducing new product concepts.

587. Break the Rules

Classical advertising, as taught in marketing and advertising textbooks, is not entirely applicable in the rural markets. The principles of advertising need major adaptations, for application in the rural markets in the Third World. There should be no diffidence in breaking the rules laid down in textbooks.

Preparing a Rural Advertisement

588. Unique Selling Proposition (USP)

The Unique Selling Proposition of a product, must be identified and emphasised, based on the characteristics of the villagers.

589. Advertising Appeals

The appeals used in rural advertisements should harmonise with the characteristics of the rural target audience, at whom the product is aimed.

590. Emphasise the Logo

Due to the levels of illiteracy, rural consumers often identify a brand by its logo. They seek the brand, by its logo when they visit the grocery store.

591. Just One Message

An advertisement aimed at the rural consumer, should not be cluttered. It should have just one basic message. This message should ideally incorporate the central product benefit.

592. Relevant Story

The story on which an advertisement hinges, should be relevant to the lives of the villagers, and should be a "slice of their lives".

593. Product in Use

Whilst advertising products on TV, it is useful to demonstrate their actual use by the consumer. It carries conviction.

594. Use of Colour

Villagers love bright colours. Rural advertising and publicity media lend easily to colours, e.g. wall paintings, banners, TV commercials, etc. Bright and gay colours should be chosen for rural advertising.

595. Deploy Rhythm and Music

Music and folk-dances are an integral part of rural life. They cut across barriers of caste, class and income.

596. Language Preference

Advertisements for the villages, should be in regional languages.

597. Film Stars as Models

Film stars enjoy tremendous popularity in the villages. Villagers identify closely with the screen feats of their favourite matinee idols. They make popular models for brands. Thus film starts in rural advertising are a major draw.

Pricing in Rural Markets

598. Pricing Vital

The price of the product, is a critical determinant of the fate of a product in the rural market. The market shares and volumes of the company, are influenced significantly by the price.

599. Pricing –Rural Marketing Tool

Price revolves around two elements - utility and value. Utility is the generic property of the product to satisfy a need. Value is the perceived worth, the consumer attaches to the product, for which he is willing to pay. In the buying process, both the utility and the value factors play a role.

600. Pricing Goals in Rural Markets

The pricing objectives and strategy in the villages of a company, depend on a number of factors, viz. the marketing and financial goals of the company and the life cycle stage of the product. The key goals of pricing in rural markets are (1) Increase sales volumes, (2) Maximise profits, (3) Achieve Target Return on Investment, (3) Maintain competitive pricing, and (5) Ensure stable prices.

601. Increase Sales Volumes

Most companies in the rural markets are keen to increase sales volumes rapidly. To achieve this, they are sometimes willing to accept lower margins. The price has to be low, to attract a large number of buyers.

602. Maximise Profits

The goal of pricing in the rural markets could be to maximise profits. This is possible only when the product is an early entrant in the villages and has no competition. Profits can be maximised if a manufacturer is able to offer a truly unique product or a technological advantage.

603. Target Return on Investment

A company enjoying leadership in a product category can pursue the goal of earning a certain rate of return on the investment in the business.

604. Competitive Pricing

Most companies operating in competitive rural markets are pragmatic enough to appreciate that they can exercise only a limited influence on market prices. They therefore, try to be in alignment with prevailing competition prices.

605. Stable Prices

A manufacturer could pursue the policy of stable prices, for sustained spells of time to build a market for a product in rural markets. The company would hold prices to improve market shares.

Variables Determining Rural Prices

606. Estimated Rural Market Size

Prior to determining the price of a product, the company must estimate the total size of the rural market. The company needs to study the price elasticity of demand of the product, to establish a linkage between the price of the product and the likely sales.

607. Psychological Price

The company also needs to ascertain the price that the village consumers psychologically expect to pay for a product. Rural consumers are not naive.

608. Target Share of the Market

Companies are now increasingly able to tailor their pricing policies, to obtain target market shares. A company that seeks to expand its market share, may have to keep its prices lower than that of the competitors.

609. Competition Policies

A key variable in determining the pricing of a product, is existing and potential competition pricing policies and practices.

610. Trade Margin Expectations

The margins expected by the rural distributors, wholesalers and retailers also impact the price of a product. The company should ideally determine the margins charged by various associates in the distribution chain.

Non-conventional Marketing Strategies

611. Grass-Roots Level Marketing

Sales and marketing activities which establish direct contact with consumers and bypass traditional selling and distribution routes can be termed as "Grass-Roots Level Marketing".

612. Bicycle Brigade

A bicycle would have a trunk or plastic box, fastened or soldered at the rear. The bicyclist salesman would fill three to five cartons of small packs of detergents, toilet soaps, sachets of margarines, hair oils, tea packets, etc. in the trunk. He would then visit 30 to 40 tiny outlets, selling one to three dozen sachets or packs, etc., to them. His daily sale would be around USD 100.

613. "Storming the Streets"

"Storming the Streets" is a promotion to contact over 10,000 consumers directly in the streets and sell them a brand. For instance, the proposal may be to sell tubs of cooking fat, directly to consumers in a town over four days. A staff of 100 salespersons would be required for this purpose.

614. 100 Mothers Selling Programme

The objective of "Mama Mia" programme is to place a product into thousands of homes through direct selling. This modus operandi was used to get quick trials and penetration of products in a country. The 100 housewives formed a semi-permanent auxiliary field force for the company, hence the designation: "Mama-Mia" operation. (In Swahili, the word "Mama" means a Mother and "Mia" means 100.)

* * *

"You can take a horse to the water, but you cannot make him drink it", is a plebeian home truth. A consumer can be motivated to visit a shop, through advertising and sales promotion, but he cannot be compelled to buy the brand.

Merchandising can clinch the issue and motivate the consumer to buy the brand.

* * *

10

Merchandising To Boost Sales

615. What Is Merchandising?

The word "merchandise" means goods for sale. Merchandising is a comprehensive concept, which embraces, all activities at the retail level, to promote the sale. All activities in the shop of a retailer, which are designed to speed the movement of product from the retailers' shelf to the shoppers' basket, are termed as merchandising activities.

616. Merchandising, a Trigger

Merchandising of products is a key trigger of sales in hypermarkets and millions of small groceries and shops, across continents.

617. Fight, Fight

"I'm too tired to answer. I can only think about it. I get energy by looking into the future and seeing what defeat will mean. Other fighters have been defeated more than I've been, but they have amnesia. They forget the lesson. I never forget it."- Mohammad Ali, Legendary Heavyweight Boxer. Merchandising is like a punch in marketing.

618. Last Punch and Communication

Merchandising is the last burst of energy, that "last punch", in marketing which makes the difference in winning or losing a consumer. Advertising and sales promotion can make a customer aware of a product and generate a desire for it. It is merchandising, which motivates a consumer to buy a product.

619. A Universal Discipline

Merchandising of products is crucial across selling formats. A village corner store, a small town grocer or a hypermarket in a city, all need to merchandise their products, to augment sales. Merchandising as a discipline cuts across size, type and format of retail outlets and even countries.

620. Merchandising: Essence

Merchandising is the essence of good salesmanship.

621. Celebrities also Merchandise

Even celebrities have to merchandise themselves. The well-dressed movie stars at the Oscar ceremonies, like Jennifer Lopez, adorned in fashionable designer gowns, are also merchandising themselves, for image impressions of themselves.

622. Selling and Communication

All selling activities can be summarised in one world "Communication". The word communication comes from the Latin word "communis", which means "common". When we communicate with anyone, we are essentially establishing commonness with that person. Merchandising is a way of establishing commonness or communicating with the consumer.

623. Horses and Water

"You can take a horse to the water, but you cannot make him drink it", is a plebeian home truth. A consumer can be motivated to visit a shop, through advertising and sales promotion, but he cannot be compelled to buy the brand. Merchandising activity, however, can clinch the issue and motivate the consumer to buy the brand.

624. Elements of Merchandising

Merchandising consists of two key elements, the imaginative use of Dealer Service Material (DSM) and the alluring display of products in a retail outlet.

Therefore, a piece of Dealer Service Material is not merely a piece of cardboard or paper or tin. It is essentially a medium for communicating a message about the product.

625. Rural Merchandiser

In the rural markets, at the weekly "peeth" (market), the village merchant displays all his products on a sheet on the ground i.e. bangles, trinkets, hair-pins, cosmetics, etc., to allure the farmer's wife. This village merchant is also merchandising his products.

626. Hawker Merchandiser

The ballpoint pen hawker, outside Churchgate railway station in Mumbai, who stands the whole day and screeches ceaselessly, "Air India pen Rs. 11, Air India pen Rs. 11," is also merchandising. Anyone who wants to sell anything has to merchandise, irrespective of the fact whether he is selling a product or service, though the style and form may vary.

Advantages of Merchandising

627. Silent Salesman

Merchandising offers innumerable advantages to a company. When a customer visits a retail outlet, his attention can be allured by an attractive display of a new brand, thus increasing awareness about it. It complements the selling efforts of the company.

628. Support Advertising

Merchandising provides a significant support to the advertising campaign.

629. Goodwill

The time spent in merchandising and displaying stocks at the store, builds tremendous goodwill in the marketplace.

630. Brand Switching

Merchandising gives a fillip to brand switching.

631. Inventory Control

Merchandising and product displays also contribute to managing inventory levels in a retail outlet, through a systematic rotation of stocks.

632. Impulse Buying

The imaginative use of DSM in a retail outlet can lead to impulse buying by consumers. Impulse buying is on the increase, since many consumers have surplus income.

633. Supermarket Counters

Supermarkets and hypermarkets cluster many items near the check-out counters to spur impulse buying, as the customers pay their bills. Stores place candies, chewing gums, batteries, blades, etc., at the check-out counters to remind customers to pick up these items.

634. Merchandising Retailer Benefits

New products and promotions move faster and the sales are brisk, when there are good product displays. Certain shops are able to charge a premium, because the products are kept tidy and presentable.

635. Buying Process

Merchandising accelerates the buying process, since it reminds the consumer to buy a product, when he sees its display in a shop. The consumer also becomes aware of new products and promotional packs through effective displays.

Types of Displays

636. Product Displays

Product Displays should be attuned to the type of outlet and the profile of the regular clientele. There would be no point in having a product display of premium branded perfumes, in a shop in a lower-income locality.

637. Image Displays

Image Displays are used to underscore the image of the product in a visual manner. This display supports the theme, message and the advertising effort of the company.

638. Scheme Displays

Scheme Displays are used when a special discount or incentive is being offered to the consumer. Such displays are used to rivet the attention of the consumer on the special discounts being offered.

639. Signature Displays

Signature Displays can also be used effectively to highlight the benefits of a product.

640. Eye Level

A display should be conspicuous and dominant, to arrest the attention of the consumer who visits the retail outlet and should be at the eye level. It should be at a spot where there is maximum consumer traffic.

641. Retailer Fees

The practice of charging a fee has become so widespread, that a large number of retailers are reluctant to display the products of a company until they derive some financial benefit.

642. Future: Merchandising Discipline

Merchandising and displays are being treated as vital disciplines, not merely by large companies, but even by small companies. As the range of products increases and the expectations of consumers augment, the competition for the retailers' shelves will also intensify.

* * *

To manage a business during conditions of protracted strife, a business leader should have a stout and warm heart, a financially hyperactive mind and nerves of steel.

* * *

11

Business In An Embattled World

643. Learnings in a Civil War

a) Survival when almost everything is against you,
b) Endurance, when there is serious danger,
c) The criticality of building strong armies,
d) Avoid regional social and economic imbalances,
e) Avoid religious strife,
f) Value of good governance and leadership,
g) Surviving, when hungry, forsaken and lonely,
h) What short sightedness does in societies,
i) Not to lose,
j) Not to give up, ever.

644. In Distress

Pain, agony, hurt and betrayal: Love them! Be a black cat commando, emotionally and physically! Define an agenda, and move. Set a goal, and meet it, daily, weekly. That way, anyone can keep sane and sensible.

645. Detrimental Impact

When political strife grips certain areas for protracted spells of time, it has a detrimental impact on the overall economic growth of the region. Existing companies are unable to grow rapidly and entrepreneurs are wary of investing in such areas. Management teams lose long term perspective, since they are involved daily with tactical fire-fighting operations.

646. Sales Decline

The primary impact of sustained strife is on sales. Sales can atrophy, or stabilise, either due to a reduction in demand or due to migration of people as a result of the hostilities in an area.

647. Demand Cycle

The demand cycle for products can undergo cyclic changes, due to extended strife e.g. curfews, shutdowns, roadblocks, etc. Consumers tend to over-stock during political and social disturbances. Uncertainty results in changes in attitudes of retailers and consumers and their buying patterns.

648. Credit Policies

Changes in demand patterns also lead to pressures on credit policies. In a situation of uncertainty, the general tendency is to keep a tight rein on money. The shopkeeper reduces his credit to the customer and the distributor cuts his credit to the trade.

649. Maintaining Quality

Business must also ensure that the quality of their products, is not compromised, even though the market is ready to absorb anything available. Situations of strife frequently lead to shortages and there is a temptation to compromise on quality. Companies of repute sustain exacting product standards despite hurdles.

650. Working Capital, Commercial Impact

Prolonged strife has significant ramifications on the commercial function. There is an increasing demand for credit and financial incentives, which have to be monitored. Working capital also merits vigilance, because it can literally go haywire.

651. Communications

Communication arteries comprising of telephones, e-mail services, postage services are also under pressure, compelling businesses to be more agile.

652. Cost Monitoring

Costs need close monitoring, during periods of strife. There is a tendency to overlook costs and go for results, with scant attention to budgets. Costs should be controlled rigorously to counter the temptation to get things done "at any cost whatsoever".

653. Production Declines

Production can be detrimentally affected in disturbed areas, due to frequent closures, necessitated by riots and curfews. Production can also suffer due to stock-outs of raw materials, unless inventory levels are rigorously monitored.

654. Pivotal Role of Personnel Function

During periods of strife, the personnel function has a very crucial role to play. The prime task of Human Relations, (HR) is to ensure the safety of the employees and maintain their morale at a high level.

The concern of management for employees should be translated into specific actions, which facilitate their operations and ensure their safety.

655. Management Leadership

During periods of curfews and unsafe travels, it is necessary for senior management to spend more time with the field force to boost their courage and morale. The salespersons should see that their leaders and managers are not petrified to travel and take risks.

656. Insecure Conditions

An employee, who is beset with personal anxieties and concerns, does not shed them off, when he punches his attendance card at the factory gate. He brings his concerns to the machine on which he works. Managers must endeavour to reduce the anxieties amongst the employees, so that the latter are productive and positive.

657. Avoid Soft Options

The softest option, which many weak or smaller businesses may adopt, is to move out their operations from the areas of strife. This would be extremely damaging to the business in the long run. The softest option is invariably the worst option in the long-term health, of an individual or business.

658. Managing the Business

To manage a business during conditions of protracted strife, a business leader should have a stout and warm heart, a financially hyperactive mind, and nerves of steel.

659. Long Term View

The eyes and vision of the business must be on the distant horizon, to an era when the political and social discord will cease. For, as Dag Hammarskjöld, the former Secretary-General of the United Nations wrote, "Never measure the height of a mountain till you have reached the top. Then you will see how low it was."

* * *

Strategic planning does not produce miraculous results overnight. Formal corporate planning will be a critical necessity to grow and survive in a competitive environment.

* * *

12

Corporate Planning, Vital Priority

660. Human Judgment Vital

Corporations undertake strategic corporate planning as a formal discipline. Corporate planning is a qualitative exercise, demanding rigorous analysis and sound judgment. Quantitative tools and models, are essentially supports, to sharpen analysis and refine judgment. There is no substitute for informed human judgment.

661. Strategic Decisions

Strategic decisions involve the structuring of the resources of the firm to ensure maximum returns in the long run. Planners have to analyse numerous factors and their impact on the firm e.g. existing business of the firm, government policy, strengths and weaknesses of the organisation, existing and potential competition, product market opportunities, resources strategy, etc. Strategic decisions must be distinguished from operating decisions.

662. Government Policy

The critical variable in corporate planning is to determine the attitude and industrial policy of the government. It is necessary to make realistic assumptions about government policies. This requires close and constant monitoring of government thinking and policies.

663. Competition Review

The quantum and type of competition in the market, is an important variable in corporate planning. It is difficult to estimate the total impact of any new competition because data about new projects, capacity utilisation, may not be easily available in entirety or may not be dependable.

664. Choice of Technology

Choice of technology has also to be reviewed along with technologies being used by competitors and market trends. The technology being deployed should not become obsolete in the near future. The choice of technology should also have the flexibility of upgrading through innovations.

665. Qualified Manpower

The availability of adequate and competent personnel to execute corporate plans should also be weighed. High quality professionals may also opt to be self-employed as entrepreneurs, consultants, etc., due to higher financial rewards and professional satisfaction.

666. Market Information

Collecting accurate market intelligence, poses another issue in corporate planning due to the paucity of relevant data and information. One way to overcome the paucity of information is to commission special surveys through research agencies, though these can be time consuming. Investment and merchant bankers are also major sources of market information.

667. Changes in Market Structure

Manifold variables impact the structure of the market, i.e. growth in real incomes, inflation, prices of housing, employment opportunities, etc. They cause changes in demand. A corporate plan is based on catering to specific market segments. However, market segments can change in size and characteristics.

668. Financing and Funding Patterns

A critical area in any corporate plan is determining the funding. The sources of funds, has a significant impact on the costs of the business. The key decision is: whether the proposal should be financed through "internally accrued resources" or through external borrowings or through public funding.

669. Money and Strings

An important decision is the determination of the proportion of funding from financial institutions. They may increasingly demand higher representation, in the operational management of the enterprise, which they fund.

Institutional funding will also mean that the debt equity ratio will be governed by the government or quasi-government agencies. Businesses may increasingly rely on internally accrued funds, for financing corporate plans.

670. Rural Markets Growth

Rural markets are galloping in developing economies like Brazil, Nigeria, India, Vietnam, etc. Rural prosperity has a significant impact on the demand for agricultural products, consumer products and eventually for industrial products. Demand in the rural areas is a function of irrigation and electrification plans, trends in agricultural production, monsoons, etc. Lack of adequate data about rural markets, may however pose a problem.

671. Social Responsibility

Business organisations across the world will have to be prepared to accept social audits and scrutiny from the government, press and the public. Corporate plans should therefore be tested on the anvil of social contribution.

672. Social Objectives

A business organisation is a part of the milieu in which it operates. Its objectives should be in harmony with the goals of that society. A corporation can pursue social objectives like development of a new township, investing in backward or tribal areas, imparting functional skills to local labour, etc.

673. Estimate of Time Factors

A principal reason for the failure of many strategic plans is over-ambitious time targets for projects. Even the most realistic time estimates can go haywire, due to delays beyond the control of executing teams.

Delays in acquisition of land, delivery of plant and machinery, especially if it is being imported, etc., can lead to delays. Whilst preparing time budgets, it is provident to provide adequate buffers for unforeseen contingencies.

674. Avoid Tight Schedules

It is also vital to guard against the temptation of setting tight time schedules, as a challenge to the implementing team. This can result in demoralisation if they are not realistic.

675. Management Responsibility

Corporate planning is a key responsibility of top management. It cannot be delegated or divided. The chairman and the board of directors normally undertake corporate planning. Task forces in functional areas assist the board.

676. CEO Influence

Whilst the CEO must influence the direction of growth and take the final decisions, he must ensure that his aspirations and operating style do not impede an objective assessment of reality.

677. Time for Corporate Planning

The key task of top management is to map the future course of the business. Top management will have to consciously make time for corporate thought. Time for corporate planning will have to be spent in large blocks and not in minor driblets, to do justice to the exercise.

678. No Overnight Miracles

Strategic planning does not produce miraculous results overnight. Formal corporate planning will be a critical necessity to grow and survive in a competitive environment.

* * *

The functions of planning and control are perceived as Siamese twins. While planning helps in understanding and reducing the uncertainties of the future, control helps to monitor the implementation of projects on a planned basis.

Planning is the soul of managerial activity. However, it is not an end in itself. A plan must be operational and must work. A plan is like a blunt tool, if it does not deliver.

* * *

13

Role Of Planning

679. Basic Purpose of Management

The primary function of management is "to make, two blades of grass grow, where only one could grow." Basically it means maximisation of results through intelligent allocation of scarce resources.

680. Role of Planning

Swedish economist Gunnar Myrdal saw planning as a tool for rapid economic advance. Sir Arthur Lewis, Nobel Prize winner, viewed it as an instrument to maximise results from scarce resources. And Billy Goetz, President Massachusetts Institute of Technology, considered it as "fundamentally choosing between alternatives." The most simple definition of planning is deciding what to do, how to do it, when to do it, where to do it and who will do it.

681. Key Management Function

At the highest level managers devote 50 to 70 per cent of their time to planning for the future. At the middle and junior levels managers should devote about 20 to 30 per cent time to planning. While the planning at the highest levels is strategic in nature, the planning at the middle levels would be operational and tactical in nature.

682. Siamese Twins

The functions of planning and control are perceived as Siamese twins. While planning helps in understanding and reducing the uncertainties of the future, control helps to monitor the implementation of projects on a planned basis.

683. Time Spans

An enterprise can draw long, medium and short term plans. While the actual time span is relative to each enterprise, most long-term plans encompass 10-15 years, medium-term plans refer to 5-10 years and short-term plans refer to a time-span of less than five years.

684. Short, Long Term Blend

Short-term plans should be integrated with long range planning. Having defined the long-term objectives for the total enterprise, it is possible to set sub-objectives for shorter time spans.

685. Goals and Good Plans

A good plan clearly defines the goals of the enterprise. It should also be flexible enough to incorporate changes, due to fluctuations in the internal and external environment.

686. Prerequisites for Sound Planning

Planning is a conceptual activity and requires the intellectual skills and strengths of the manager. It has to be based on accurate information, sound judgment and sensitivity to the environment.

687. Eternal Vigilance

Like liberty, planning also demands eternal vigilance! Vigilance is assured through feedback, procedures and systems.

688. Pride of Place

Over the years, planning has come to occupy a place of pride in management, because it helps to frame a strategy for the future.

689. Planning Must Deliver

Planning is the soul of managerial activity. However, it is not an end in itself. A plan must be operational and must work. A plan is like a blunt tool, if it does not deliver.

* * *

The sensitive manager cannot neglect the informal side of the organisation. This is the pattern of relationships that evolves among employees, over a period of time. It cuts across official and formal relationships. Any endeavour to eliminate, bypass or overrule it, will result in tension. The objective of the manager should be to use the formal and the informal paradigms to achieve organisational goals.

* * *

14

Decentralisation And Organisation Structure

690. Inordinate Centralisation

Inordinate centralisation can lead to over-burdened executives taking decisions under pressure. Morale and motivation can suffer since executives at middle and junior levels may feel neglected and uninvolved.

691. Young Managers

Young professionally trained managers are an ambitious, aggressive lot. They demand responsibility and accountability at early stages in their careers.

692. Apparent, Actual Decentralisation

It is necessary to distinguish between apparent decentralisation and actual decentralisation. An organisation may have all the paraphernalia, which characterises a decentralised organisation like delegation procedures and controls. However, in practice decision-making may be highly centralised, depending on the personality of the leader.

693. Family Businesses

Many family business houses have decentralised the production and marketing functions. However, the finance function is rigorously controlled by the family members. Such organisations are characterised by a pervading tendency to look to the superiors or the owners of the business, whenever there is an emergency.

694. Criteria, Organisational Structure

A sound organisation structure is based on the basic principle of delegation of responsibility. The natural corollary is that there can be no responsibility without authority.

695. Division of Tasks

The first principle impacting organisation structure is the systematic division of functions and tasks, keeping in view the abilities, skills and attitudes of the employees. Hammering round pegs in square holes, can make an organisation ineffective.

696. Span of Control

The span of control of any manager should ideally not exceed six to eight individuals. The lines of authority must be clear, within and between departments and managers, to prevent confusion or friction.

697. One Boss Rule

Unity of direction implies that the briefing to a manager, must come from a single source. If an individual receives his instructions from more than one source it creates problems in reporting, resulting in loss of time, energy and morale.

698. Dynamism Essential

An organisation has to be dynamic enough to perceive new opportunities in the environment for growth, expansion and diversification.

699. Informal Organisation

The sensitive manager cannot neglect the informal side of the organisation. This is the pattern of relationships that evolves among employees, over a period of time. It cuts across official and formal relationships. Any endeavour to eliminate, bypass or overrule it, will result in tension. The objective of the manager should be to use the formal and the informal paradigms to achieve organisational goals.

700. Decentralisation Is In

Decentralisation of responsibility is essential to ensure participation and commitment of the employees.

701. How much Decentralisation

The degree of decentralisation in an organisation is a function of the ownership pattern, attitudes of senior management and the capabilities of the team.

702. Ideal Organisation

An ideal organisational structure permits free communications between team members, besides avoiding any conflict due to overlapping of authority.

* * *

Control is not a magic password, which unlocks the doors of results and performance. Controls have to be administered judiciously.

* * *

15

Management Control Process

703. Why Control?

An organisation sets certain goals, in quantitative or qualitative terms. Control mechanisms are deployed, to ensure that whilst achieving these objectives, there are no deflections from the planned routes. Control processes can compel events to confirm to plans, through regular rectification of deviations.

704. Good Control System

A good system of control, contributes to detecting course deviations, before they take place. The effective control system should be anticipatory in character. It should ring the alarm bell, before a problem materialises. In the ultimate analysis, effective controls, like good management, should deal with problems before they arise.

705. Three Steps in Control Process

The first step is the establishing of appropriate standards. Standards are generally quantitative in character but may also be qualitative. The second step is the measurement of actual performance against the standards. Mathematical and statistical tools are deployed. Budgets are the most common form of accounting tools. The final step is management action designed to correct the deviations from established norms.

706. Criteria for Good Controls

A good control system should report the deviations in the operations promptly, to save resources and capitalise on opportunities. The control system should be forward looking. It should highlight the exceptions at critical points and also the areas that merit attention and action. Controls should be flexible and economical to administer. The cost of administering controls should not exceed the gains that ensue.

707. Establishing Controls

In establishing control systems, two major variables merit serious attention. First, the system must be simple to operate and should be sparing of manpower. Second, most human beings resent being controlled and this can cause behavioural problems. Both these issues need to be managed adroitly.

708. Lucid Communication

The basic purpose of control is rarely understood or appreciated. Controls are essentially methods to identify areas that need correction, to achieve the organisation's goals, in a cost-effective manner. The purpose of control should be lucidly communicated to those who are impacted by them.

709. Control Is not Magic

Control is not a magic password, which unlocks the doors of results and performance. Controls have to be administered judiciously, through the use of tools and techniques.

710. A Budget

A vital tool of planning and control is the budget. A budget is a periodic and quantitative expression of the goals of the organisation. It manifests the objectives of the enterprise in financial terms.

711. Sense of Balance

Inordinate controls can stifle initiative and imagination. However, inadequate controls can lead to a decline in standards and eventually to demoralisation in an organisation.

712. Bureaucracy and the File

In a bureaucracy, management of issues and individuals is not based on whims but on predetermined procedures and written statements. The "file" becomes a critical storehouse of precedent and memory.

713. Advice from Abraham Lincoln

The great American statesman Abraham Lincoln once said, "What is the use of running, if you are on the wrong road?" If an organisation is clear as to where it is headed, it will proceed more swiftly and economically. Sound control systems can help.

* * *

The countries we are posted to, have survived without us for centuries and done well. Many of them have performed better than us. Therefore, we should avoid landing up as "messiahs of wisdom". We should be humble.

* * *

16

Enjoying Expatriation

714. World, Global Village

As the world becomes a global village, professionals travel across countries and continents to work in suitable international assignments. Professionals follow work, wherever it may be. Fresh challenges await every expatriate.

715. Comfort Factor

Managers, who work for 10-15 years in established multinationals and business houses, in their own countries, get habituated to a work culture and ethic. Many managers become stars in their own companies.

716. Yesterday Is Dead

A foreign posting changes everything. The expatriate manager starts his career again, from a scratch. Yesterday's conquests stand wiped out, after one flight to a new country. It is like joining a new company as a management trainee.

717. New Country and Culture

An expatriate has to adjust to a new country, where the language, customs and food habits are new and exacting. Imagine being a vegetarian, posted in Latin America, having to learn Spanish and not being able to get a vegetarian meal, surviving on sandwiches or pizzas for months.

718. The Cost Factor

However bright an expatriate manager is, many local managers will always ask, "Do we really need him? A local manager is being deprived of a job!" Expatriate managers are normally paid more than locals, in lieu of the hardship and separation from the family.

719. Delivery Counts

In a global economy, results, delivery and merit will eventually be at a premium, irrespective of nationality.

720. New Mountains

Expatriates have to conquer new mountains! Tough, but great fun, because it invigorates you to commence a new inning after working for 10 to 15 years in your home country. The challenge is to establish one's reputation quickly.

721. Be Utterly Professional

Even when superiors or colleagues behave in a depreciating manner, do not compromise your esteem and values. Your self-respect is in your hands. Firmly, but politely adhere to professional standards of conduct and etiquette.

722. Delivery and Respect

The world respects results. Whatever the circumstances, avoid self-pity, depression or pessimism. Focus on results. Deliver the plans, irrespective of the additional work or sacrifice it takes. Then respect will follow.

723. Share Credit

The best way to win the confidence of local teams is to share credit generously, to the extent of giving away credit for one's own contributions also. Local managers are not looking for foreign "heroes". They are looking for colleagues who contribute.

724. Adapt, Adapt and Adapt!

Accept the cultural work-habits of the country gracefully. Learn to work with and through local managers. Do not impose your own values too strongly on new subordinates. Let them recognise your worth over a period of time. Then, they will cooperate.

725. Humility Works

The countries we are posted to, have survived without us for centuries and done well. Many of them have performed better than us. Therefore, we should avoid landing up as "messiahs of wisdom". We should be humble.

726. Learn, Learn

Before we commence preaching, we need to learn ourselves. We must respect the language, values, habits and leaders of the new countries. Otherwise, the local teams will reject us instantaneously.

727. Be Patient!

In a globally networked world of ours, thoughts and words travel at the speed of lightning! However, attitudes yet change very slowly. Beliefs change over centuries. Therefore, an expatriate manager has to be patient, with himself, his team and his environment.

728. Give Pride a Backseat

Ideas that may have worked in domestic markets, may not deliver abroad. So, never carry an argument to a breaking point, based on the experience in your home country. An expatriate manager should avoid making any discussion, a make or break decision.

729. Accept Some Loneliness

When you arrive in a new country, initially, there are no friends, mentors, well-wishers and confidants. They have to be built again. So, one has to learn to manage being alone and lonely at times. (You could spend a Christmas alone in a hotel, because you do not have personal friends in a new country! So what? Read a good book!)

730. Resolve Family Matters

All family issues should be resolved before accepting a foreign assignment. For instance, your spouse may be a working professional. How will a foreign posting impact her/his job or career? Perhaps you also have children studying in schools or at university. How will a foreign posting impact their education?

731. Management of Discrimination

Despite the efforts of the entire world to ensure an equitable world, the fact remains that we always encounter some discrimination everywhere based on colour of the skin, eyes, hair, country, religion, etc. There could always be some discrimination in some part of the world, in some form or the other. Expatriates have to learn to live with it and manage it.

732. Learn and Enjoy

All foreign postings are great learning experiences. One learns about one's own limitations, inabilities and inflexibilities. Therefore, we grow as persons, after going through the ordeal of adjustment. You learn about new markets, languages, people, cultures, festivals, forests and rivers.

Eventually, managers who have received global exposure will emerge as better professionals and persons. The future belongs to them, because the corporate world is gradually becoming a global village.

* * *

Managers cannot be isolated from the environments they operate in. The new Managers will have to be concerned about social justice and equitable distribution in our society. They will have to be concerned not merely about building businesses but also focus on banishing hunger and poverty.

* * *

17

Managers And Society

733. New Concerns

Managers cannot be isolated from the environments they operate in. The new Managers will have to be concerned about social justice and equitable distribution in our society. They will have to be concerned not merely about building businesses but also focus on banishing hunger and poverty.

734. New Pattern

The world will increasingly be technology driven. Industrialisation will flourish in Asia and Africa. Urbanisation will drive into villages. However, vast parts of the world will remain poor. The continued existence of poverty on a vast scale will produce tensions in society. Disparities in wealth and incomes should be a concern to the new managers, since inequalities will create social frictions and disturb markets.

735. Man-Management Proficiency

The manager does not merely have to possess technical skills. He has to be proficient in man-management skills also.

736. Government Management

Future manager-leaders will also have to work in greater collaboration with Government and local authorities on business issues. They will have to develop the attitudes and skills required to deal with these institutions on a continuous basis.

737. Principles and Privileges

A society that sheds its principles will soon lose its privileges too.

738. Involved Citizens

The awareness and sensitivity of citizens to political affairs are likely to augment. There will be increased participation by citizens in social media forums and the political process. Public opinion will be more organised and vocal and will have a determining impact on government policy and action.

739. The Family Ties

The family will continue to play a major role in societies, determining attitudes and living styles. Urbanisation and industrialisation will lead to a weakening of traditional joint family ties. Individuals may get weaned from joint families and form nuclear families.

740. Corporate Social Responsibility

Businesses can consider:

a) Opening of schools, so that children of the weaker sections can receive vocation-oriented education, either free or at a nominal charge.
b) Provision of clinics and medical services, so that the poor are not disabled or weakened due to lack of medical attention.
c) Institution of community centres, where recreation and sports facilities are made available to the economically weak, to nurture their talents.

741. Sensitivity to Society

The new manger will be effective if he contributes not merely to his organisation but also his society. The manager cannot insulate himself from the socio-political processes that are shaping the values of the citizens. The courses in management institutes could provide opportunities for comprehensive discussions of the political and social processes. Higher social sensitivity will make the manager more relevant.

742. Community Involvement

Management students should also be encouraged to involve themselves actively in rural community work. For instance, a business school may adopt a village and make it a model in terms of education, literacy, housing, health, recreation, etc. The development of the village could be on phased basis, with groups of 10-15 students visiting it annually to deliver specific projects. This will make the students aware of rural issues.

* * *

You are being interviewed from the moment you enter the employer's premises. Anything you do or say, which may be seen or heard, will influence the judgment. The astute interviewer will study your body language also.

* * *

18

Great Job Interview

743. Talk to Company People

Talk to current employees to get a lucid picture of the cultural ethos of the company. Then assess the type of person the company would be looking for during the interview. Companies look for functional competence in new recruits, but they are also concerned about the "cultural-fit", i.e., the value system of the recruit. Talking to existing employees is useful to determine your cultural alignment with the company.

744. Attention to the Application Form

The interviewer should get a good feel about you, even before meeting you, from the application form. It generates the first impression on the employer, which could also be lasting and conclusive. A first good impression is a valuable asset, in a competitive situation. Application forms constitute the basis of the questioning. Highlight your strengths. Then, bat on a wicket of your creation.

745. Wear Formal Clothes

Dress up formally. Wear a white shirt. One candidate wore a brand new pair of shoes at an interview. The shoes kept on pinching and distracting him. The interviewer realising his dilemma, requested him to remove his shoes. At an interview, it is vital to be comfortable with oneself. It is important to dress up formally, but be relaxed.

746. Be an Early Bird

It is best to reach about 15 minutes before the interview, so that there is enough time to find the location, straighten your tie and get a "feel" of the place. This will build confidence and improve performance at the interview.

747. Anticipate Questions

Questions normally fall in the following categories:

a) Testing conceptual skills,
b) Examining functional competence and knowledge, and
c) Reviewing attitudes, aptitudes and personality.

List all the questions that can be asked. Then, no question or interview can surprise you.

748. Plan Your Answers

It is critical that the replies are compact, concise and relevant. If you have thought through the questions and the structure of your answers, you will give pithy replies.

749. Steer the Interview

Steer the interview to underscore your strengths. Be alert and agile, like a tiger. Guide the interview towards your strengths. The reply to a question frequently forms the cue for the next question. Successful candidates "guide" their interviews.

750. Do Not Bluff

Never, ever, try to bluff through such questions, however strong the temptation may be. Good companies place a very high premium on honesty and character.

751. Look in the Eyes

While answering questions, look the interviewer in the eye. Always, establish eye contact.

752. Be Alert

You are being interviewed from the moment you enter the employer's premises. Anything you do or say, which may be seen or heard, will influence the judgment. The astute interviewer will study your body language also.

753. Time to Think Through

A candidate could also be asked questions about which he has not thought through. Ask the interviewers for a few moments to think, formulate thoughts and reply. The maximum time should be about 15 to 20 seconds.

754. Ask Questions

Prior to the conclusion of the meeting, interviewers give the candidate an opportunity to seek clarifications. This opportunity can be used to strengthen one's position by asking relevant questions. If there is no real question, just thank the panel. Then, go.

* * *

A manager does not get trained automatically merely by attending a training course; he has to consciously work to derive the maximum learnings from it.

* * *

19

Art Of Attending Training Courses

755. Employees Are Assets

Most companies are realising that their employees are valuable assets. It is people who manage all the other resources. Hence, increasingly companies are focussing on training their staff, through internal and external programmes.

756. Who Is Attending?

It is useful to enquire directly with the organisers and determine the level of other participants. At one course, the brochure was ambiguous. Thus, the finance director of a large company found himself grouped with managers at least two levels below him. He left after the first session, relieving his own embarrassment and the tension of others.

757. Get the Material in Advance

Request the organisers to send the study material in advance. This gives an opportunity to go through the course material thoroughly. Having obtained the study material in advance, time must be consciously budgeted for study.

758. Focus on the Course

Leave your job behind you. No job can be performed satisfactorily by remote control. Apart from being unfair to the company paying for the course, interruptions disturb other participants.

759. Identify the Core

Many speakers tend to cramp their presentations with jokes, anecdotes, etc., to captivate interest. It is vital to identify the central point and not get bogged down by jokes and anecdotes.

760. Training at Harvard

Training is hard work. Harvard is a monastery! Wake up at 5.30 am, exercise; breakfast at 7 am, classes from 8 am to 5 pm. Dinner at 6.30 pm. Then, living-group homework between 8 pm and 11 pm. Later, revise next day's case studies.

761. Harvard's Long Term Associations

Harvard Business School training programme participants normally become lifelong friends and associates, across the world. HBS fosters and encourages its Alumni to keep in touch with the College and with each other, through a range of programmes and events on an ongoing bass.

762. Harvard and Books

Read, collect, buy all books the faculty recommends. Books are wealth. My surprise at Harvard Business School: Young clergyman John Harvard, whose name the university bears, did not donate much money; he bequeathed £779 (50 per cent of his estate), and 400 books! Thus, the Harvard logo, "Books Tell the Truth!"

763. Assimilate Lessons

Attending a training course, by itself does not contribute to the effectiveness of a manager. It is vital to assimilate the lessons learnt and then blend them with operational practice.

764. Grain or Chaff

When a speaker speaks too much or too long, learn to separate the grain from the chaff.

765. Mental Gymnastics

A manager must use his mind actively and constantly, to evaluate the practical applications of the concepts being discussed.

766. Practise, to Benefit from Training

A manager does not get trained automatically merely by attending a training course; he has to consciously practise the art of getting the maximum benefit from a training programme.

767. Avoid Shallow Participation

The management schools have coined the term "C.P." i.e. Class Participation, which frequently degenerates into verbosity. At training courses there are no evaluation grades. So, it is not necessary to talk to score brownie points.

768. Use Silence

At times, silence can be more eloquent than verbal participation.

769. Mingle and Talk

At external programmes, the maximum knowledge comes from other participants, during informal chats. Meet as many of them as possible, on a personal basis. Some of the personal relationships, established at these courses, prove to be valuable lifelong professional associations.

770. Tea, Coffee, Talk to Participants

The meal and coffee breaks should be used for moving around and meeting people, on a personal basis.

771. Walk, Walk, Walk

It is useful to take long walks during the breaks to exercise and also have a change of scene. This refreshes and improves receptivity.

At Harvard, six weeks and 2,500-page readings later, my eyes were red, swollen. Then, I would sneak out and take long walks in the lush-green lawns of the campus, dodging the darting squirrels and turkeys. Later, I was ready for more case studies.

772. Read All Material

To derive the maximum benefit from the training course, specific time must be budgeted to read and digest material, which is relevant and could contribute to effectiveness on the job.

773. Action Plan

At the end of each session one should identify one or two key action points, which can be translated into practice on the job. Avoid too many action points and trying to implement them in a hurry at the same time. It is best to accord priorities and bite as much as one can chew.

774. Just Two or Three Action Points

When we finished our Advanced Management, eight-week programme, at the Harvard Business School, Professor John Kotter, a leadership expert advised us, "You may have picked up 7,000 ideas here. Just focus on one or two. If I meet you anywhere in the world, I will only ask you, "What are you doing with your life?"

775. "What Is Your Life?"

That was a lesson: what are we doing with our lives? Do we matter in the lives of the poor and the weak? Marketing, finance, production teach us to sell shampoo, shoe-polish, shaving-cream. How do we build a better community and leaders who make a difference?"

776. Let the Mind Wander

The liberation from routine is the best time for letting the mind wander and evolve original ideas. Many a knotty problem has been resolved, by a manager letting his mind wander and incubate, whilst attending a training programme.

777. Ask Questions

Asking questions and seeking clarifications improves perspectives and also contributes to learning. Moreover, questions also contribute to breaking monotony and making the participants mentally agile.

778. Check about Notes

Check with the speaker whether he intends distributing a synopsis, after his session. In case he does not have a paper to distribute, you can request him, to prepare one for distribution to all the participants.

779. Use Cards for Making Notes

It is a useful practice to make notes on post-card sized ruled cards, which can be bunched together and preserved. They are compact and make for easy reference.

780. Change Your Seat

One of the techniques of avoiding fatigue and monotony is to change your seat as often as possible. This will help you to get to know more people.

781. Get the Addresses

Obtain the list of all the participants, to enable you to keep in touch with those participants you wish to know better.

782. Avoid Similar Programmes

Unless there is a specific need for revision, attending a similar course too soon, is a sheer waste of time, energy and money.

783. Training Programmes Can Bond

In eight weeks, 150 students from multifarious continents interwove into a stout community. We willingly gave up preferred pleasures, to keep the team bonded. The minds exercised, but the hearts ruled. The 900 hours of hard academic labour at Harvard, where we learnt, above all to live in harmony with students from 55 participating nationalities, irrespective of ideology or religion, forged us into caring friends, alumni.

If this lesson had been widely disseminated, then we could have saved the four precious lives lost in the 15 April 2013 Boston bombings.

* * *

Business trips are frequently undertaken at short notice and packing is done hurriedly. To ensure that you do not forget all that you may need, it is important to have a checklist of the items that you may need.

Many frequent travellers maintain a separate wardrobe for travel. This travel bag is always kept ready. The clothes and items in this bag, are not used on a daily basis.

* * *

20

Productive Business Travel

784. Travel: A Must

Touring has become an integral part of a manager's job. Though sophisticated information and communication systems are now available, there is just no substitute for on-the-spot assessments and human judgment. CEOs, board members and senior managers also tour, to ensure that they are familiar with operational realities.

785. Be Ready

Imagine you are getting ready to meet the Prime Minister of a country or the Chairman of a company and you find that the collar button of your starched white shirt, is missing. So, it is clever to check what you have to wear next morning, before sleeping the previous night.

786. Travel Checklist

Business trips are frequently undertaken at short notice and packing is done hurriedly. To ensure that you do not forget all that you may need, it is important to have a permanent checklist of the items that you may need. Many frequent travellers maintain a separate wardrobe for travel. This travel bag is always kept ready. The clothes and items in this bag, are not used on a daily basis.

787. Avoid Carrying Cash

A definite way of avoiding anxieties on a business trip is to avoid carrying large sums of cash. It is safer and convenient to use traveller's cheques and credit cards. If one does have to carry cash, it is best to carry it in two places, e.g. your wallet or briefcase, so if either is lost or stolen, you are not stranded.

788. First Aid Kit

Carry your own first aid kit, which should include remedies for ailments like coughs, colds, digestive upsets, minor burns, cuts, etc. During a tour, one is exposed to a variety of climates, water and foods, which could have an unpredictable impact. The medical kit will also be useful in the villages, where the nearest doctor could be hours away.

789. Extra Change of Apparel

It is provident to carry an extra set of clothes in case the business trip gets extended. It is infuriating to start a fresh day in stale clothes. An extra set of clothes does not really add substantially to the baggage. I always carry an extra set in my hand luggage. This has proved useful, whenever my checked-in baggage is delayed.

790. Check the Room

It is useful to survey the room on checking into a hotel. Some travellers do not like rooms, with interconnecting doors, even though they are locked. Other travellers, do not like heights; hence, they prefer rooms on lower floors. Such requirements should ideally be communicated to the hotel in advance.

791. Confirmed Bookings

It is always useful to travel with confirmed bookings throughout the itinerary. This reduces uncertainties and tensions.

792. Maintain Accounts

The smart manager keeps a separate book to maintain his accounts on a tour, so that he can prepare his expense statement expeditiously on return.

793. Reading Material

During trips, a lot of time is wasted in waiting for flights, hotel rooms, appointments, etc. This time can be deployed profitably to catch up on reading. Some managers regularly set aside interesting books and articles, which they read on tours.

794. Identification Tags

Ensure that all the bags have a tag, with the name, address and telephone numbers. In case the baggage is misplaced or left behind, it will make it easier for the airlines to contact you.

795. Understand the Local Ethos

Travelling is a useful opportunity to educate yourself about the towns and villages that you visit. A manager, who travels a lot, has an opportunity to understand the diversities that make a country.

* * *

Always maintain a sense of balance. You may work for a big or grand company. Remember it is not yours, unless you own the majority shares. However much your bosses exhort you that it is your company, remember it is not. If you are the proprietor of a business, even a 100 per cent owner, remember someday the enterprise will pass on to your successors. We really do not own anything permanently, in this world.

So, always make time to laugh and be merry. Laugh a lot. Then, you will achieve more.

* * *

21

Epilogue

796. Let Money Chase You

Pursue ideas and customer-service. Render the best customer-service in the world. You should never have to chase money. Instead, pursue excellence. Then, money will chase you.

797. Always Be Enthusiastic

Pursue your goals with a smile and enthusiasm. Enthusiasm is the petrol of life. Just as a car is immobile without gasoline, life is hopeless without zeal.

798. Look in the Eye

Look in the eyes of the people, when you talk to them. People do not trust leaders with shifty eyes. Focus on people when you are with them. Do not be distracted. When a person is with you, give him your complete, undivided attention. Great leaders have the capability of making you feel very important, when they talk to you. President Jimmy Carter talks to you in a crowded room and makes you feel that you are the only person in the room and the most important person in the world to him. This is Leadership.

799. Break the Walls

Never take "No" for an answer. If you are confronted with a wall, jump over it or circumvent it. Or, just make a hole in it. Continue progressing. People, who achieve, defy defeat ceaselessly.

800. Win Friends, Not Arguments

Win friends, not arguments, in the office or in the market. If you win an argument, you will be happy for an hour. If you win a friend, you will be happy for the rest of your life. If you ever need help later, a victorious argument will not come to your aid. A friend will.

801. Be Kind to the Staff

All of us are not born with the same privileges and benefits. So always be kind to people who have not had the opportunities, advantages and benefits that some have been bestowed with.

802. Never Act Out Of Prejudice

We do not decide in which caste, community or country we are born. It happens. So always be fair. Do not hold people's skin or hair colour, community or nationality against them. Stay with merit and performance.

803. Never Humiliate Anyone

Every person, even if he is a peon, cleaner, driver or a waiter has self-esteem. Respect everyone. Never demean anyone, even when the performance is poor. Pull people up, even reprimand if necessary, but do not hurt their pride. If you humiliate a person, he will wait for retribution. Then, that humiliation will become his strength.

President Donald Trump took office as the President of USA, the most powerful nation in the world, in January 2017. According to TIME magazine (27 April 2017), at a White House Correspondents' Dinner, "The skewering of Trump did not end with Obama — Seth Meyers, host of the dinner that year, took aim at the Trump for several minutes, complete with an imitation of the future president. The scathing remarks did not sit well with Trump, who was filmed looking angry, with his lips pursed and eyes staring ahead.

Media and political pundits have since said that the White House Correspondents' Dinner roasting was what spurred his run for the presidency in 2016."

So, avoid humiliating anyone.

804. The Rule of Five

Planning helps you to deliver more. Every night, before I sleep, I make a list of tasks to be accomplished the next day. The list could run to 15 to 20 chores. Of these, I tick five. These are the most important items, which are "Must-Do". These tasks should be completed, whatever happens, even if there is a tsunami or a storm. The process helps me to address the most important issues daily.

805. One-third, Two-third Ratio

Ideally never spend more than one-third of your salary or earnings. Save two-thirds. In business too, whether your business earns USD 100 or USD 100 million, restrict spending to the bare minimum and save or invest the balance. You will rejoice in the long run with this formula.

806. Always Be Honest

We are human beings. We can think. So, we must live by some values. Remember what the Bible teaches, "For what shall it profit a man, if he shall gain the whole world, and lose his own soul?"

807. Always Keep the Boss Informed

If you are working for a company, you will always have a boss. Even if you are the chairman or the CEO, you will have a boss. You may be reporting to a Board of Advisory Directors. Or, even the Government. Always keep the boss informed of any major adverse deployment, whether it is personal or official. Bosses hate shocks. It is better if they learn about setbacks from you, rather than from the press. If you take them into confidence, they may even protect you.

808. Keep a Bit Detached

Always maintain a sense of balance. You may work for a big or grand company. Remember it is not yours, unless you own the majority shares. However much your bosses exhort you that it is your company, remember it is not yours. If you are the proprietor of a business, even a 100 per cent owner, remember someday the enterprise will pass on to your successors. We really do not own anything permanently in this world.

So, always make time to laugh and be merry. Laugh a lot. Then, you will achieve more.

809. Best Lemonade in World

Suppose you land up just getting some lemons in life. No problem. Make the best lemonade in the world. Be the best of whatever you are, in the world. If you are just a cobbler in the world, make the best shoes in the world.

810. Get the Best

"It's a funny thing about life.....if you refuse to accept anything but the best, you very often get it". Somerset Maugham, British writer.

811. Care for People, Genuinely

Be genuinely interested in people. Their personal affairs may not be the concern of the organisation. However, if you can help some person or guide him in a human crisis, he will be eternally grateful and loyal to the organisation too. After a career of 45 years, the best bosses I remember and celebrate are the ones, who guided or advised me, when I was going through tough times, officially or personally.

812. Make Time for Personal Concerns

Always try to help your team members, if they have a personal issue. A young couple in my company had a child, which fell ill one night. Their neighbour was a company General Manager, Mr. D.B. Patel. He took out his car and escorted the couple and the baby to a hospital and spent the entire night with them, to ensure the child was fine and the parents were reassured.

Always enquire about the health of the parents, spouse, and children of your team members. An office is more than a place of work. It is also a social organisation, where people lean on each other during adversity.

813. Promise Less, Deliver More

"Always promise less and deliver more. Always, ask for more time to deliver, then deliver ahead of schedule," was a wise counsel I received in 1969, from Professor Dr. K. R. Maheshi, Head of the English Department, Sydenham College of Commerce & Economics. I have tried to follow his advice and have never been let down by it.

814. Quite, Quiet

Every day, spare about 30 minutes to pause and reflect about the direction of the business. It is important to be quite quiet, at times.

815. The Business of Credit

At times you may find you are not getting credit for your contributions. Others are walking away with the bouquets and trophies. Keep cool and patient. It is a matter of time, when people notice your efforts. Never get bitter. Bitterness is corroding and destructive.

816. Enjoy Business, Enjoy Life

We are all guests in this world, with temporary visas. So build a business, knowing fully well, that we all go without a farthing from this world. So, enjoy building a business and the wonderful life that it offers, knowing that we build for future generations, to take it forward.

817. Fight One More Round

"Fight one more round. When your feet are so tired that you have to shuffle back to the centre of the ring, fight one more round. When your arms are so tired that you can hardly lift your hands to come on guard, fight one more round. When your nose is bleeding and your eyes are black and you are so tired you wish your opponent would crack you one on the jaw and put you to sleep, fight one more round – remembering that the man who always fights one more round is never whipped."- James Corbett, American Professional Boxer.

818. Avoid Shortcuts in Life

Real and lasting success always comes from hard thinking, work and sacrifice. So, do not waste time seeking shortcuts to success or glory.

819. Follow Your Heart and Intuition

"Your time is limited, so don't waste it living someone else's life. Don't be trapped by dogma - which is living with the results of other people's thinking. Don't let the noise of others' opinions drown out your own inner voice. And most important, have the courage to follow your heart and intuition." - Mr. Steve Jobs, Co-founder of Apple INC.

820. Believe and Conquer

Remember, they conquer, who believe they can. Napoleon Hill says, "What great achievements has he to his credit, who says it cannot be done?" And Roger Federer adds, "If you believe, you can go really far in your life."

821. Enjoy the Sunset and Rainbows, Too

If you want to succeed in any business, you must approach your desk every morning, with a fresh mind. So in the evenings or the weekends, enjoy the majesty of mountains, beautiful sunsets, colourful rainbows, fragrance of flowers, etc. Rejoice and live each day anew.

Never Give Up

When mountains of trouble tumble down,

When the loyalty of friends has disappeared,

When those whom you helped try to shun you,

When those of whom you expected something slink away,

When those basked under your glory deceive you,

When those whom you made avoid you,

When those whom you admired doubt you,

When the thorns outnumber the flowers,

When those who preached principles betray them.

When you are saturated with shocks,

When the body refuses to take another step,

When the devil of pessimism knocks persistently at your door,

When the darkness of the night seems everlasting,

When the spirit tells you it has fought enough,

When everything is at its lowest ebb,

It is then,

Then, that you must not give up.

The path may be long

And the bare feet may bleed,

The tears may pour down incessantly,

And the heart may be as heavy as lead.

It is then, that you must not give up.

It is then, that you must not complain,

For he who complains accuses himself.

Every night has a day following it,

Every deep river has a bank on the other side,

After the rains come the rainbows,

And after the pain comes the healing.

By Hari Chand Aneja

Available on Amazon

By Hari Chand Aneja
Available on Amazon

Also by Rajendra K. Aneja
Available on Amazon

Also by Rajendra K. Aneja
Available on Amazon

Also by Rajendra K. Aneja

Available on Amazon

Also by Rajendra K. Aneja
Available on Amazon

Also by Rajendra K. Aneja

Available on Amazon

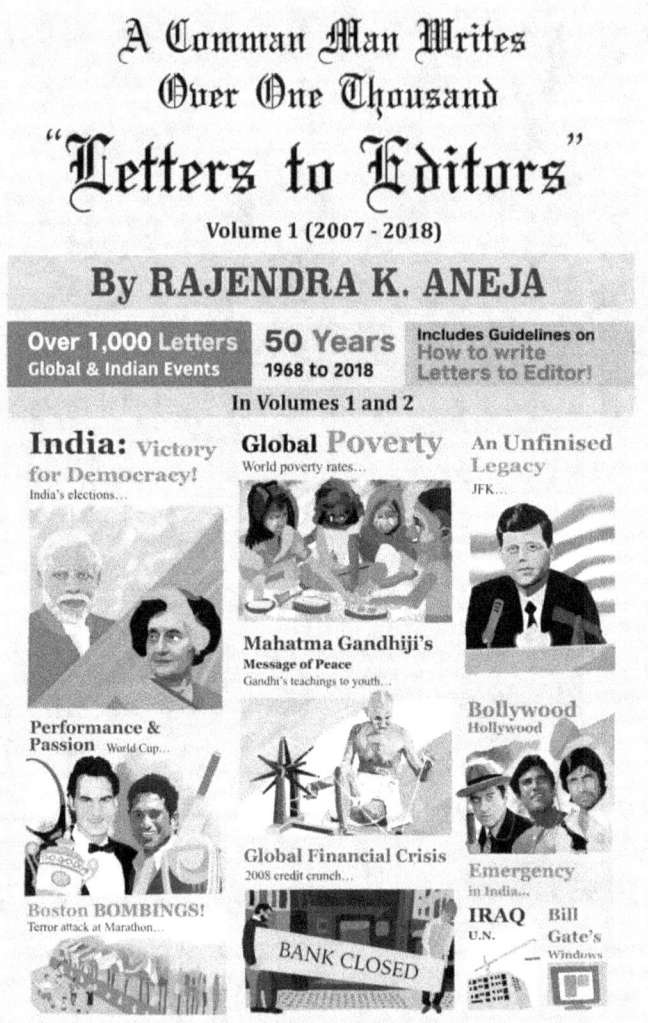

Also by Rajendra K. Aneja
Available on Amazon

Also by Rajendra K. Aneja
Available on Amazon

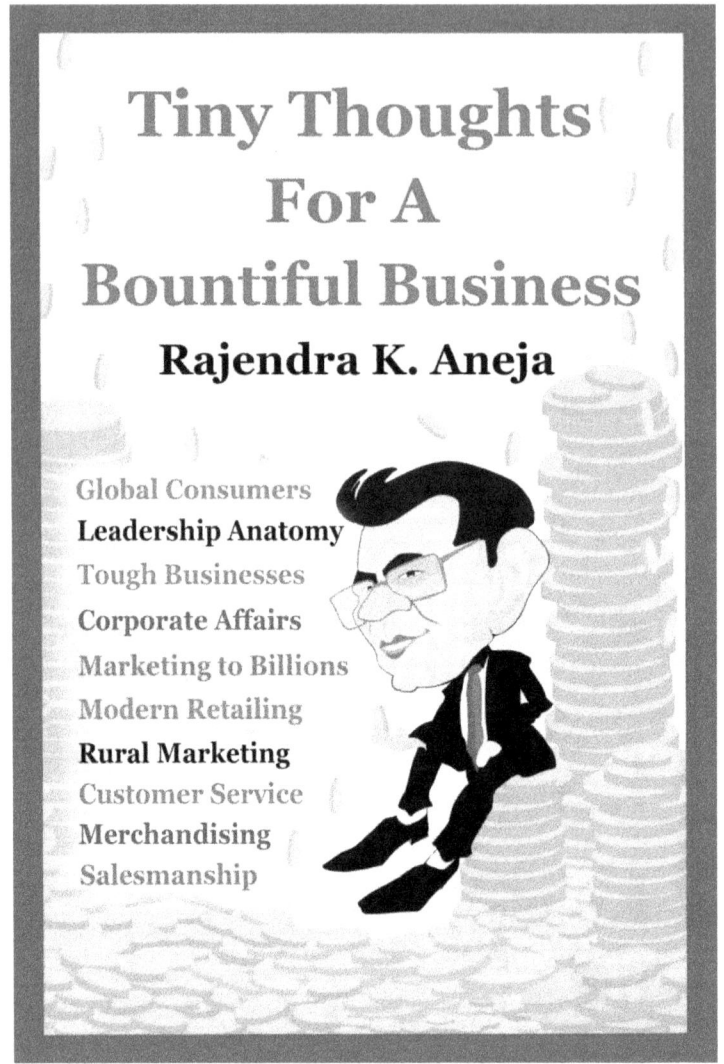

By Rajendra K. Aneja
Available on Amazon

www.ingramcontent.com/pod-product-compliance
Lightning Source LLC
Chambersburg PA
CBHW071249220526
45468CB00001B/51